a gaggle of
ONE

a

soaring symposia

gaggle of
ONE

by
Gren Seibels

Some Notes on this Book

The text was set in Journal Roman typeface on the IBM
Composer. The book was composed, printed and bound by
LithoCrafters Inc., Ann Arbor, Michigan.

Jacket design and maps by Trudy Seibels.

Unless otherwise credited, all photographs by the author.

SOARING SYMPOSIA

408 WASHINGTON ST.
CUMBERLAND,
MARYLAND 21502

This book is affectionately dedicated

to the memory of my friend and teacher,

ABBOTT COTTEN MARTIN

who never flew, but whose mind soared.

Well, then, it comes down to this. There are two kinds of men, those who live for appearance and comfort, and those who live in a world of raw realities slugging their way to the graveyard proud, and sinking their teeth in life like it was Kansas City sirloin medium rare. The members of the group who go for Sunday afternoon drives with the kids and bowl on Thursdays can't for the life of them understand how the others ever busted loose. They know why well enough, but of course they won't even admit that much, the most of them. They talk as if they're perfectly satisfied with the squirrel-cage routine of life at the office and the Elks; and, by God, pretty soon they are satisfied. Meanwhile, cousin Slim, who was "always kinda harum-scarum," or brother Bill, who "was pretty erratic as a kid," is slogging the seven seas in rusty old tramp steamers, laying pipe line across the Persian sands, building bridges, booming oil in Manitoba; or, close to home, railroading or steamboating or pulling the transports across the plains, and sucking in a hundred dollars' worth of fresh air a minute. I guess it boils down to those who thrive on taking chances and those who turn pale at the thought. You'll never get past those city limits, boys, unless you just up and go.

Richard Bissell

The Monongahela

CONTENTS

Page

PREFACE

Flying sailplanes cross-country has filled some of the least monotonous hours of my life. Whether under the pressure of competition or simply for fun and practice, these flights frequently supply moments of private melodrama—in some cases, more than I would really prefer. Occasionally, after flying myself into a particularly nasty bind, I begin wondering what a *real* pilot would do in such a fix. The question is moot, of course; real pilots never let things get so badly out of hand.

In conventional aircraft, we overcome gravity and other natural inconveniences with brute horsepower, boring a noisy hole in the sky and boasting that we have conquered the air.

The soaring pilot learns to collaborate with nature, rather than subdue it. He gratefully accepts lift, not necessarily where he wants it, but wherever he finds it. He must develop sensitive reflexes that instinctively respond to subtle suggestions from natural forces touching wing and rudder, aileron and elevator. He must court the sky, not rape it. As these basics are acquired, soaring opens to the neophyte a hitherto secret world of beauty and grace and freedom, along with the warm companionship of others who have shared the discovery. And here, many pilots are content to draw the line: happiness is at cloudbase, just an easy glide from the home field.

Yet—a machine that can climb on sunpower and then glide considerable distances poses for some of us an irresistible invitation to the high adventure of cross-country soaring. On even the most modest and leisurely excursions, the pilot is pitting skill and judgment against known factors of gravity and drag and adverse wind, along with such unknowns as sinking air or a wildcat strike in the thermal factory. Every cross-country is flown at the risk of a forced landing—until we are on final glide to our destination, with altitude to spare.

If we choose, we can fly very conservatively, making slow progress but cutting the risk factor to the vanishing point; or we can go hell-for-broke, rejecting all but the strongest thermals, with perhaps a new speed record at the end of the line—or a broken sailplane. In soaring, as in no other sport, we are free to set whatever degree of challenge we are willing to accept.

The ultimate challenge is flying in competition. When a soaring pilot is ready to know truly how good (or how bad) he is, competition offers the most reliable yardstick. Perhaps, after consistently beating all the local 1-26s to the tops of local thermals, an innocent might enter his first contest with a sense of complacency. By the end of the first task, his confidence is apt to be shaken; by the end of the second, it should be demolished. But at least he will now be in the proper frame of mind to begin his serious education. And when it's over, he will realize—like hundreds of pilots before him—that in these few days of intense competition, he has learned more about soaring than during all his previous flying. Chances are he will also know more about himself—both good and bad—than he ever did before.

The pilot with the greatest potential regards himself essentially as a student throughout his flying career, for there will always be more questions than answers. To a soaring pilot, the sky is like a fascinating book being written faster than he can hope to read it. In that unique world, gravity is the only fixed certainty; all the rest is speculation, hope, hunches and optimism. Altitude is our sole security, and often damned hard to come by. We eventually realize that we fly, not so much against others —competitors—as against ourselves: our personal frailties of mind and eye and hand and spirit.

I have been flying, off and on, for 35 years; the flights I remembered to log total more than 2000 hours. Yet before every takeoff, I still regard what is about to happen with a student's diffidence and an amateur's awe. I have always been overwhelmed by the pure wonder of flying; I still can't take it for granted.

At the beginning of every contest, I am also over-whelmed by the caliber of the soaring talents with whom I have presumed to compete. I consider soaring pilots the élite of the flying world; and competition pilots, the *crème de la crème*. We rejoice, Trudy and I, in this superb company of airmen—a most select family, bonded not by chance of blood but through a shared awareness of the secret sky. Like us, many of them enter contests with no rational expectation of winning, but for the supreme challenge and joy of flying as hard and as well as possible against the finest in the sport.

Sharing the risks and exhilarations of aerial competition with other pilots and their devoted crews creates a rather wonderful rapport, much like that between fighter pilots who fly together in combat—a bond as unique and noble as anything in life, and quite beyond the power of words to depict. I only allude to it here lest everything else in this book still fails to explain why our sport grips us in happy thrall until we grow too feeble to climb in or out of a racing cockpit.

It seems clear to me, now, that when I wrote *Pilot's Choice* (1970), I must have been mining a large vein of enthusiasm with only a small trowel of experience. Only three years a soaring pilot, I still nurtured many of the beginner's simplistic notions about the sport. No sooner was the book published than I blithely set to work on a sequel, all about competition. As the pages accumulated, however, so did experience. Reviewing this material later on, I realized that my ideas were changing with every contest I flew. A viewpoint that once struck me as sound, even profound, would appear quite daft a season later; most of those essays wound up in the trashcan.

This updating process might go on indefinitely; not only am I still learning, but the sport itself is so dynamic, so rapidly evolving, it won't stand still long enough for any description of it to be called definitive. Either one sinks in a morass of perpetual revision, or one declares a cut-off point. Arbitrarily, perhaps boldly, I have decided on here and now.

Therefore many of the comments on equipment, contest rules and so on may seem quaintly obsolete in a short time. To me, at least, these matters are peripheral to the soaring people themselves, and their stories—subjects that really interest me. It is in these areas that I hope I have been lucky enough to capture some of the flavor of the sport as we know it in the mid-1970s.

By the way, if you were hoping for a book about how to win soaring contests, there are some very good things in print, but this is not one of them. With a respectful bow, I leave that sort of thing to the competent types who regularly *win* contests, which has not precisely been my forte. In countless outings, I have managed to win just one Regional championship; and that, if you would believe my faithful detractors, was patently a fluke.

On the whole, what I have attempted is to describe, from the cockpit point of view, some of the glories and tribulations that exalt or beset the average competition pilot. If you bothered to keep score, you would note a roaring disparity between the brief glories and the endless tribulations; so be it. The entire sport is an affront to common sense; we fly against imponderable odds, with unpredictable vexations always lurking just ahead.

While the pressures spring from different sources, soaring-for-records has much in common with contest flying. In both cases, something on the order of ten-tenths performance is the minimum for any chance of success. To illustrate, I have wandered from the contest circuit to the Appalachian ridges in one maverick chapter, and to wherever memorable events took place, in others.

Some soaring people are such ultra-purists that they disdain all other modes of flying with the starchy hauteur that true sailors reserve for powerboats. Not I; while contest soaring tops my priority list, I delight in almost any form of flight that qualifies as sporting—*i.e.*, useless. To this end, we own a beautifully restored 1931 Great Lakes biplane with which I regularly frighten myself blind while trying to recapture some of the aerobatic sequences I once learned as a young Navy pilot. So there's one chapter in which sail-planes scarcely get a mention; ultra-purists may have to skim it.

Like any sport worthy of our serious attention, soaring is rooted in the admirable human impulse to learn, to grow, to overcome, to excel. Its special flavor derives from the unique combination of natural and human factors upon which it is based—among them, weather and terrain, altitude and speed, observation and judgment, skill and intelligence, timing and luck, risk and caution, and—yes—courage and fear.

In describing the responses of certain pilots to these challenges, it seemed appropriate to use some of the short-hand language of soaring. Lest these terms should mystify pilots who don't soar, or laymen who don't fly, I have resorted to a few footnotes to help clarify the jargon.

It is idle to expect objectivity from a man in love. I am
much in love with this sport of soaring; and while I have
tried to describe it honestly in these pages, I am aware that
there is much beauty in the eye of the beholder. At any
rate, in competition the scoresheet ranks us with the harsh,
impersonal objectivity we can never bear to apply to our
own performances. Those ruthlessly accurate numbers are
not influenced by memories of long hours in a cramped
cockpit. . . of fast glides punctuated by visits to cloudbase
aboard whooshing thermals ... or of that curious
compound of tedium and terror that accompanies a long
grind at pattern altitude in a hesitant thermal that won't
organize itself, watching an anonymous farmer tractoring a
nameless field, wondering if he would mind a sailplane
landing along his meticulous furrows ... The scoresheet
simply reports, with mathematical indifference, that we
came in eleventh for the day.

I can recall no soaring flight which, in retrospect, could
not have been improved. Oh, there have been a few—a very
few—which could not have been improved a great deal. It's
not much of a record, after more than 1300 soaring hours
in pursuit of that will-o-the-wisp, perfection: a dozen of
those hours, or possibly fifteen, when I felt myself in total
harmony with the sky, sensing thermal cores seconds before
the variometers confirmed them, instinctively finding blue
streets paved with zero-sink, effortlessly stringing together
chains of good decisions.

All too rare; but once tasted, never forgotten.

Gren Seibels

Columbia, South Carolina

1975

LONER'S GAME

Suddenly a pilot's voice breaks through the squelch on the finish line radio:

"Zero Bravo two miles out!"

The timer reaches for his mike and acknowledges, "Zero Bravo, roger," and joins the other contest officials scanning the horizon for a glimpse of the first finisher.

Hours ago, the last of the racing sailplanes streaked across the starting line and disappeared off in the July haze, beginning the first leg of a 200-mile triangular speed course. Now the sun is only an hour or two from the western horizon, but there are patches of ground still hot enough to spit powerful thermals[1] into the sky.

An eagle-eye at the start-finish line soon spots the white speck, low over the trees, moving very fast. A thin plume of spray trails back from the ship's belly—the pilot is dumping his water ballast. In eerie silence the knife-edge wings and bulb-shaped fuselage hurtle toward the officials' tent at 150 mph.

Then comes the rushing, whistling protest of still air being parted by several hundred pounds of man and fiberglass moving at 220-feet-per-second, slanting down to zero altitude. Leveling off in the turbulent ground effect, the

---

[1] Thermal: a column, or elongated bubble, of rising air which derives its energy from heating of the earth's surface, as by sunlight, large fires, or industrial furnaces; the *sine qua non* of soaring flight over flat terrain. Usually invisible, unless generated by a violent dust-devil, thermals often form cumulus clouds at their tops—valuable (but not infallible) guides in locating lift. If a thermal is so weak it barely offsets the sailplane's rate of sink, so the ship neither gains nor loses altitude while circling in it, the polite term is "zero sink."

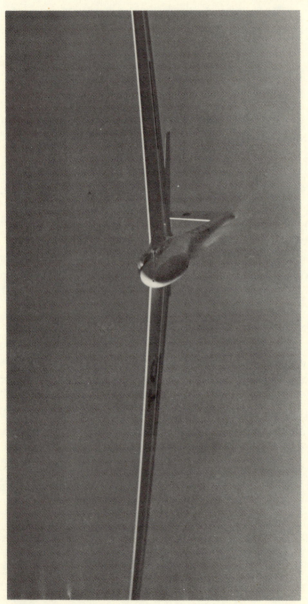

A THIN PLUME OF SPRAY TRAILS BACK FROM THE SHIP'S BELLY . . .

Hurtling across the finish line at placard speed, racing pilot drops some 150-pounds of water ballast from wingtanks prior to landing. Ballast increases wing-loading, which in turn improves high-speed glide ratio; but it takes its toll in climb efficiency, so water is carried only on strong thermal days.

plane flashes across the finish line, so low over the grass that anyone standing nearby can look *down into* the cockpit. The timer calls "Hack!" from his sightline, and an assistant—staring at the official chronometer—notes the precise hour, minute and second of the finish.

The sailplane is already curving steeply back into the sky, the jetlike roar muted then gone as the pilot reconverts speed into altitude.

"Good finish, Zero Bravo," says the timer into his mike.

"Thank you, sir," acknowledges the pilot, lowering his mainwheel with a soft "Clunk," then floating around a lazy pattern to a delicate landing, slowly rolling out toward his trailer which waits beside the runway.

At intervals during the next hour, many more ships come hissing home, often in clusters of three and four, strafing the finish line with water ballast, gracefully flaring off to left and right, sorting out their own traffic with a casual nonchalance that would turn the hair of a professional controller.

It is quite a show.

Competitive soaring at its best is a loner's game. To stay in contention, each pilot must handle each task in his own way, forming his own strategy, applying his own tactics; in the near-silence of his cockpit he concentrates with ferocious intensity on making as many right moves as he can, and as few wrong ones.

Most beginners (and a surprising number of veterans) tend to bumble around the course with no more of a game-plan than to get from one thermal to the next, trying to follow the leaders—and wondering why they can't. They will join any gaggle in sight because it's easier than hunting one's own lift, and they tend to stay with the pack until someone with explorer's instinct peels away from the top and flies point for the others. It's a pretty good way to make sure you get back home, but your average speed won't be much to brag about.

The loners busy themselves with decision-making: how long to stay with a thermal (since it's often a waste of time to top one out); weighing the cost of diverging from courseline against the potential advantage of stronger lift, constantly studying terrain and sky for subtle hints about what's going on to left and right, as well as up ahead. One of the greatest of all soaring pilots, A. J. Smith, once observed that if you want to win contests, you must train yourself to make several vital decisions during every minute of every flight. For me, this was quite a bombshell; up to that point, I had approached competition with a vague sense of respect and trepidation, but with no self-organization or discipline whatsoever. It also came to me, then, why my contest flying never came close to high efficiency before the fourth or fifth day of competition; it always took me that long to overcome the easy-going, sloppy habits of the weekend flyer. Since then, I've had no further problems with drowsiness while flying tasks.

Individualism, of course, doesn't inhibit good pilots from dropping in on each other's thermals, especially if the first ship in carries a prestigious competition number—and is climbing smartly. The risk of midair collision is greatly eased by everyone circling in the same direction. But to fly as close as possible to the powerful lifting core of the thermal, experts reduce the radius of their turns by banking at 50° or so, running just a knot or two above stalling speed, the closer ships separated by only a few feet of turbulent air—not a game for dilettantes.

Seen from the ground, it's a slow-motion ballet as one or two dozen sets of wings wheel and flash in the sunlight, climbing in graceful spirals. Inside the gaggle itself, one must fight against the seductive beauty of the thing, lest he be lulled into momentarily forgetting the business at hand.

We learn to watch only the planes above us; if they are well-flown, yet we are closing on them, we know it's time to leave the thermal, for the higher ships are evidently circling in weaker lift.

It is a peculiarity of soaring contests that each pilot starts the race at a different time—a practice dictated by the impossibility of lining up dozens of sailplanes at the same altitude and position for a race-horse start. In most forms of racing, the front-runner can tell how he's doing in relation to the others by simply looking over his shoulder; in soaring, you're never quite sure just how things are going until the race is long over and the official scores are posted. Being the first across the finish line is most exhilarating, but you still have to sweat out the later starters. (Some of the better ground crews keep private records of selected pilots' start and finish times, to compare with their own pilot's performance; interesting, but not too reliable.)

I have found competition soaring to be the most challenging form of flying this side of aerial combat. In a sense, it's too bad that most of the action is high in the sky, beyond public sight or hearing—a great aesthetic loss, like storing all the Renoirs in an attic. Yet privacy has its own special charms; when we make our blunders, it's a comfort to know that the whole world isn't watching.

Most of the visible activity at a contest gets underway soon after sunrise: sleek white fuselages being trundled out of their long trailers, followed by narrow, tapered wings and lightweight empennage assemblies. Knowledgable crews rig these components in minutes, then devote the balance of the morning to caressing the flawless, gelcoated surfaces with wet sponges and chamois-skins until they are surgically clean. Such activities as sealing the wing-fuselage junctions with plastic tape, which might cut the drag by one-percent, may strike you as nit-picking. But one-percent times eight

or nine contest days is not to be lightly given away. Each
crew observes its own rituals, always working against the
clock: all ships must be on the launch grid at least 20
minutes before the first scheduled takeoff. You can judge a
crew's efficiency by the amount of noise and commotion
they create; the best crews manage everything in
conversational tones.

For most pilots, the worst hour of the day is spent on
the launch grid, waiting for takeoff.

Awake since six or six-thirty, we have been absorbed
most of the morning with the myriad details of readying
our ships and ourselves for competition. Now, aside from a
final, redundant cockpit check, there's absolutely nothing
to do but wait. (I remember the remark of a Navy pilot,
shot down in the Pacific and finally rescued after endless
days on a tiny liferaft: "The worst thing about having
nothing to do is that you can't quit.")

The portable john alongside the runway does a rush
business from pilots with nervous bladders. There's an
occasional brief, bitter spat between a tense pilot and a
crewman over some triviality; the air around the grid is so
highly charged you can practically smell the ozone.
Amongst the tilted sailplanes, small knots of pilots and
crewmen aimlessly form, dissolve, and regroup, everyone
desperately feigning a coolness no one possesses. Here, even
a very bad joke wins uproarious laughter, since it
momentarily eases the visceral roiling deep in every gut.

Wristwatches seem to go into reverse as the hour drags
on toward eternity. Just before you decide to declare a
bleeding ulcer and retire from the field, you hear a towplane coughing itself to life, then another. Up at the head
of the line of waiting ships you can see the first half-dozen
pilots snapping on their parachutes and carefully easing
themselves into their cockpits, each tended by a solicitous
crew, some getting a dry good-luck kiss from wife or girl.

With action, time starts to move again; in minutes, you are buckling into your own chute as the line of ships ahead of you rapidly dwindles. With the canopy secured, close over your head, the cockpit temperature quickly soars as a lineboy scuttles under the nose and attaches the towline. Your crewman lifts a wingtip, leveling the ship; you signal thumbs-up and a moment later you feel the ship surge forward, quailing in the prop-blast from the towplane. First there's a breath, then a sweet blast of cool air from the ventilators as you gain speed. A slight back pressure on the stick and your plane is smoothly airborne; a yank on the gear handle and the main wheel retracts. You settle into an easy climb behind the towplane.

For the first time in many hours, you can take a deep breath.

Every contest flight I can recall has involved, sooner or later, a sort of inner game of "chicken"—featuring the timid, scared, what-in-the-name-of-God-am-I-doing-here? side of my nature locked in fierce debate with the brave, competitive fraction that boldly pays the entry fees and signs up for still more contests. Imagination makes cowards of us all: when the sailplane is down to 500 feet with no decent landing spot within reach, nor any likely source of lift, the mind's ear is prone to preview the dismal crunch of fiberglass against tree trunks or what-have-you. *Give me a thermal, Lord, and I'll be good; oh, lordy, but I'll be good!* Cockpit theology.

Off-field landings are the price of ineptitude; since none of us has yet achieved perfection, even our captains and our kings occasionally drop in on strangers. For lesser mortals, pea-patch adventures are as integral to soaring as, say, sunshine.

Pointing your sailplane into a strange field whose hidden perils you can only guess at supplies some of the hairiest

moments in all of flying. In the Eastern third of the United
States, especially, the open fields never seem to be very big;
and as you turn on final, with no altitude to spare and
hence totally committed, you may discover that what
looked so flat and smooth from above is actually on a
rather steep slant, rolling, laced with gullies, dotted with
boulders, edged with power lines, and altogether a lousy
place to land a nice sailplane.

But since there's no alternative, in you go—crossing the
power lines, you yank the spoilers[2] and/or deploy the
drogue chute, nose down until the last second, flare, hold it
off until the airspeed drops to full stall, then feel the wheel
slamming the surface as if it were part of your spine. You
barely manage to lift a wingtip over a rock when the
opposite tip grazes the overgrowth, digs in, and you whirl
90 degrees or so in a vigorous groundloop. After a couple
of terrific jolts, everything abruptly stops.

If you've been holding your breath through all this, as I
generally have, it will come out now in a great sigh of relief
(you're safely down)—and disappointment (you've blown
the task). In these few seconds you have felt your ship
undergo the profound change from a living, responsive
creature of the sky to an inert, lifeless assemblage of
fiberglass shapes; in effect, a dead bird. Your mind is trying
to catch up with the sudden physical transition, trying to
shift gears from the role of intensely busy airman to that
of proprietor of a large, helpless piece of equipment which
you have brought to this strange field.

---

[2]Spoilers: sections of the wings' surfaces which the pilot can extend into the
airstream, partially destroying ("spoiling") the lift, thus gaining some control
over the ship's glidepath to a landing spot. Also called divebrakes, since their
drag permits steepening the approach without increasing the airspeed, very
handy when clearing obstacles on the way into a small field. These devices have
been used to advantage on sailplanes for decades, yet the general aviation
industry is just now discovering them. Discussed further in Chapter 11.

Stiffly, you walk around the ship, silently praying you'll find no damage. If there *is* damage—serious damage—you may curse like a grown-up man, but inside you are so sick you want to cry. There is no one to blame but yourself.

Yes, there's also the risk of personal, bodily injury; and it does indeed happen, but so rarely that most pilots give it little thought. Nearly all accidents are justifiably ascribed to pilot error, in soaring as in conventional flying; but in soaring, the opportunities for pilot error are enormously multiplied by the very nature of the game. The more we expose our ships to the hazards of off-field landings, the greater the likelihood of disaster. Disaster, to a competition pilot, means pranging his ship out of the contest. From my casual records of contests in which I have flown, I gather that perhaps one pilot in twenty is apt to do violence to his ship during an average competition. As I recall some of the really ghastly spots where I (and others) have landed—unscathed—the breakage figures do seem remarkably low. We get away with it far more than we deserve to.

The thing that soaring shares with other weather-oriented sports like skiing, fishing and so forth, is the Man-you-should-have-been-here-last-week syndrome. The closest approach to a surefire rain-making system yet devised is to schedule a major soaring contest at a time and place where it has never been known to be wet. To cite just one soggy example, in the spring of 1973, in celebration of its debut as a Nationals site, Chester, South Carolina, produced its wettest June since the Weather Bureau began measuring precipitation. Of ten scheduled days of competition, five were flyable—just barely—and this in an area and at a time of year when local pilots have come to expect daily 600-fpm[3] lift not as a privilege but a right.

[3] fpm: feet per minute; the standard measure of vertical speed in U. S. aviation. Also expresssed in knots; one knot roughly equals 100 fpm.

Whatever the weather, however, the best pilots make the best of it. Apparently it's much easier for pilots accustomed to weak conditions to make the adjustment to stronger lift, than the other way around. I've noticed that fellows who do most of their flying over the southern California deserts, or west Texas, where 1200 fpm is considered an interesting thermal but not a great thermal, sort of come unglued when they have to contend with the 100-300 fpm days so common east of the Mississippi. Yet the lads from New Jersey, North Carolina and other eastern bogs seem to learn very quickly what to do with those big western thermals. Naturally, it's much more fun to soar on days when you can climb like a rocket and cruise like a SST, and only those with a genius for trouble fail to complete the course; but the scores are apt to be all bunched together and inconclusive. Contests are mainly won on marginal, scratchy, survival-above-all days when the average hobbyist wouldn't bother to buy a tow. This sort of thing can be enjoyed only by confirmed masochists, but it certainly tends to separate the kiddies from the grown-ups, and that's what soaring contests are all about.

The better competition pilots don't necessarily excel in the standard skills of thermaling, or piloting, or control-handling, although of course they do all these things very well indeed. Where they *do* excel is in their uncanny understanding of the sky—their ability to read it accurately, and to use this information intelligently; this, I believe, has been the most important asset of every winning pilot with whom I have flown.

So much for theory; let's go to a contest.

2

We are running southeast at 80 knots[1] from Bryan, Ohio, toward Lima—three of us working the big, flabby cumulus that emerge from the haze every four or five miles. "It's just practice!" I keep reminding myself; yet moments later I am instinctively pressing Tango Tango, my 15-meter Open *Libelle*, to pace the big AS-W 12s.

Ben Greene leads the way aboard Golf Bravo, renamed "Gooney Bird" somewhere along the competition trail; the pale gray "GB" incongruously small on the 12's vast T-tail. As always, Ben flies with easy assurance from one cloudbase to the next, zooming high into the heart of each lifting thermal core, and when the lift meets his standards, banking smoothly into a tight climbing circle.

Moments later, I try to imitate Ben's zoom and curl into his thermal. Boring in straight and fast, A. J. Smith hits the lift seconds after I do, his immaculate *chandelle* locking him into the core a scant 100 feet below.

From the ground, a sailplane gaggle looks so slow and stately, the tiny white shapes like feathers caught in a sluggish inverted whirlpool, imperceptibly diminishing until they disappear in the brassy haze. Dreamy stuff indeed.

Inside the gaggle itself, "slow and stately" will quickly drop you to the bottom of the stack. It is more delicate cut and subtle slash; holding your own in the middle of a

---

[1]knots: nautical miles per hour, favored by pilots because their charts are calibrated in nautical rather than statute miles. If you want to convert to miles per hour, multiply knots by 1.15.

sandwich composed of Greene and Smith goes something
like this:

> *Audio's[2] rising here, ease the bank a half-second
> . . . A. J.'s already done it, he's moving up on you . . .
> Ben's climb is off on the north side of the circle; tighten
> up when you get there, cut inside his circle . . . that
> damned yawstring—too much top rudder . . . airspeed 48
> knots: SLOW IT DOWN! . . . core keeps shifting south,
> FOLLOW it, you clod . . . lift has eased a couple of knots;
> about time to leave . . . Yeah, there goes Gooney Bird . . .
> cut through the center, flaps up, nose down, get back to
> 80 knots before we hit the sink . . .*

This was Sunday, the Fourth of July, 1971. We were
sharpening our claws for the 38th U. S. National Soaring
Championships, which would open the following Tuesday.

> *It was the best of times, it was the worst of times . . .
> it was the season of Light, it was the season of Darkness,
> it was the spring of hope, it was the winter of despair.*

Charles Dickens could scarcely have been thinking of the
launch grid on the opening day of a National Championships when he wrote those remarkable lines, but they do fit
the scene with eerie precision.

Two rows of sailplanes, as contest-ready as most of them
would ever be, covered nearly 1000 feet of the single paved
runway at Williams County airport. Cumulus like giant
popcorn already dotted the sky in all quadrants; every
plane that could carry water ballast was brimful. At the

---

[2]audio: an audible signal generated by an oscillator in the modern electric
variometer, which increases in pitch and/or frequency to indicate an increase in
lift, or rising air—thus freeing the pilot's eyeballs from constant scanning of the
instrument dial. The variometer itself is the basic soaring instrument: a highly
sensitive rate-of-climb indicator.

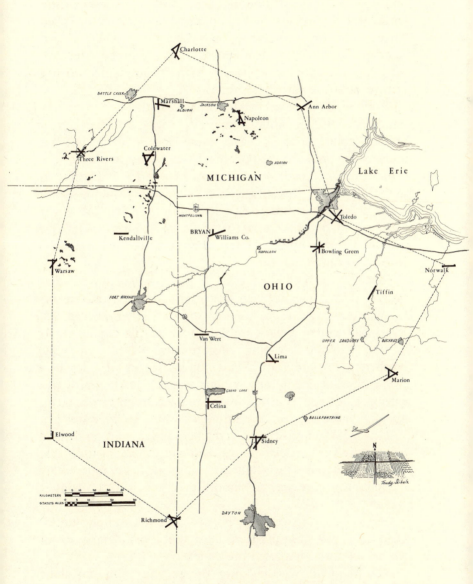

CONTEST AREA, BRYAN, OHIO

nine o'clock pilots' briefing that morning, Competition
Director Bob Jackson had announced the first task: Speed
Triangle, with turnpoints at Marshall, Michigan, and
Kendallville, Indiana; 154 miles. Chuck Lindsay, the met
man, had predicted a strong day with lift averaging 300-400
fpm to 6000 by early afternoon.

Many of us were trying to cope with the usual first-day
bundle of glitches while nervously waiting for the launch
line to open. Looking back, mine now seem trivial; but
under the pressure of Opening Day, they took on the
proportions of major calamities. After a series of frustrating
mishaps, Trudy was filling my *bota* with drinking water
when it sprang an enthusiastic leak. In tones that Job might
have envied, I told Trudy to forget the damned water; I'd
just fly thirsty. By now I was deep in jittery paranoia: the
world was out to get me.

Glancing around the grid, I grudgingly realized that
others in my vicinity had worse problems. Attaching his
heavy *Kestrel* trailer to his car for the trek to Bryan, Ed
Byars had pulled a back muscle; he was still sloping about
in the backwards-leaning posture favored by expectant
mothers. The late Dave Nees still had most of a leg in a
cast (skiing accident the previous winter); A. J. Smith was
getting feedback from an ankle sprained in an earlier meet.
My only problem, for the moment, was a leaky water jug.

Then a dozen towplanes coughed and roared, and lined
up for the first official contest launches; the confusion that
had dominated the takeoff line each practice day
miraculously gave way to smooth precision, and the contest
was on.

Concerning the task itself, my logbook simply notes:
"Cupcake"—so it must have been quite elementary; 62 of
the 65 starters completed the course.

Yet I remember going into the second turnpoint along
with Ed Byars and Ross Briegleb, all three of us losing

altitude at a sickening rate in the unexpected sink. After shooting pictures, we split in three directions in a wild scramble for lift—any lift at all. I finally found something that resembled a thermal, and the three of us milked it for a long time before venturing out on the last leg. Naturally, a mile or so beyond we ran into abundant, strong lift and had our choice of good thermals the rest of the way home. But the time we struggled at the second turn had clobbered our average speeds.

My Sunday afternoon playmates had themselves a day in their AS-W 12s: A. J. first, Ben second. Along with Dick Johnson, they would dominate the entire contest.

Glancing up at a high shelf of cirrus slowly drifting toward us from the west, Ben Greene, waiting for his takeoff, remarked: "They must have reversed the first two tasks!"

And so it seemed; with deteriorating conditions forecast for later in the day, we had been handed a long Speed Triangle, with turnpoints at Tiffin and Celina, Ohio; 222.5 miles. Yesterday the task would have been a snap; now, it appeared highly questionable as all the early launchers clustered in big local gaggles, none of which seemed to be climbing.

Things were mostly quiet at the start gate until after 1300; yet as it turned out, those who got away early fared best. Out on the first leg, I was delighted to join up with Bernie Carris and enjoy some priceless thermaling lessons as we whistled along from cloud to cloud toward Tiffin.

There I spotted George Moffat leaving the turnpoint just ahead of me. "Okay," thought I, "let's just tag along and see what the World Champion does next."

What we both did next was run through gobs and gobs of sink. Trying to pace the ballasted *Cirrus* with my ballasted *Libelle*, I kept pouring on the speed until a glance at the panel showed we were indicating better than 105 knots. With a vast blue hole opening up ahead, I felt we were spending altitude with an unseemly disregard for the occasional patches of lift through which George would zoom a few hundred feet, then tuck his nose down for another breakneck glide.

Like many before me, I mentally bade George good luck with his imminent landing and clung to the next thermal for dear life, scraggly thing that it was. After a painfully slow 1500-foot climb, I limped out on course again to find the sky completely empty of other ships. It was a lonesome moment . . . and it dragged on for at least 45 minutes as I fought to cover the long second leg and reach the Celina turnpoint before the blasted cirrus layer completely ruined the day.

Finally I began a long flat glide diagonally across the big lake that lay between me and the Celina airport; the air was lifeless. I reached the far shore with 400 feet and had begun dumping water in preparation for the inevitable landing when I felt a faint ripple along the wings. When the vario chirped for the first time in recent memory, I reflexively curled into a steep turn. If the thermal proved to be a loser, I could still just make it to the airfield.

It wasn't what we normally call a thermal; there was no core, no form to it, and damned little lift. But it's well that I studied it closely, for it set the pattern, or non-pattern, for all the lift I was to find the rest of the day. As I ground around, earning perhaps 50 feet per minute, I could see high above me a large gaggle climbing through 5000. These were my erstwhile friends from the first two legs, fat and happy. I cursed them.

After about a fortnight in that thermal, I had enough height to run in for pictures and head back north, hoping for a few more miles toward Bryan. I was joined by three other low-altitude pilgrims; we made up a squadron of four

Libelles pussy-footing cautiously homeward. It was late in the day, the overcast was practically solid, and I suppose we were all planning on a final glide to the intermediate Van Wert airport. I radioed Trudy to meet me there.

Through mile after mile of inert air, we flew in fan formation, sniffing at occasional burbles but finding nothing. Eventually the Van Wert airport appeared on the bottom of my canopy. That I could make; but a small sweep across the downwind side of town would do no harm. Carefully assessing altitude against the distance to the airport, I was in the act of banking around to land when it appeared: an honest 100-fpm thermal! Tucking in, I was instantly joined by two more *Libelles* (the third was evidently minding his own business elsewhere). Woody Woodward and young Robbie Buck were my companions, both competition veterans and close friends; I was glad for their company—until they STOLE MY THERMAL!

I still don't know just how it happened, but after a few circles Roast Beef and Whiskey One were patently out-climbing Tango Tango. I tried every trick I've ever learned; nothing helped at all. In a few minutes, they were nearly 1000 feet overhead. Paranoia was making its second appearance in as many days.

And so it went the rest of the way home. At their higher level, the lift was always stronger than at mine, and I fell farther and farther behind. However, as slow as we all were, we got back among the 59 finishers for the day—and I couldn't have been more surprised. And so goes life for those of us whose mission it is to furnish a statistical base for the winners.

Listening to George Moffat describe his flight at the pilots' briefing the next morning, I was depressed to hear him say he thought the first leg was slow (that was my *best* leg!), that he was glad he had ballast for the whole flight, and that he thought most of the pilots had flown the final

leg too conservatively—he had buzzed home from Celina at
90-100 knots, all the way. Was George really talking about
the same task, the same day?

A. J. Smith had earned another 1000 points, Ben Greene
was still a firm second, and Dick Johnson was lurking in
the Top Ten. For us late starters, it had been a tough,
frustrating day; we could only extract comfort from the
fact that all but six of us had managed to finish.

July 8th dawned, to stretch the verb slightly, but the sky
was churning with pre-frontal murk. From the benches at
the pilots' briefing, wails and moans arose as Bob Jackson
reached for his trusty blackboard with the familiar words,
"Today's task will be . . ." Then he turned the board so
the pilots could see it. It read:

Speed Task. Turnpoints: (1) Laundromat; (2) local
tavern; (3) another local tavern; (4) rest. Cheers and
huzzahs.

A rest-day during a contest allows everyone to get caught
up on fettling equipment, hangar-flying and bull sessions.
We chatted with George Moffat—blond, tall, slender,
curiously shy with strangers (easily mistaken for cold
aloofness) . . . with a chipped front tooth which, like
Brando's busted nose, keeps him from being *too* handsome
. . . highly articulate, as befits a teacher of English literature
. . . works at his sports with ferocious concentration and
total dedication (he pursued his first sailing championship
for ten dogged years) . . . positive and blunt in his opinions,
spoken or written . . . yet in view of his superb record, one
thinks twice before disagreeing. He distrusts and despises
dilettantes, but once he accepts you as serious, he can be a
warm and charming friend.

And Dick Johnson, whose National Championships span
a quarter of a century—slim, compact, characteristically
smiling when relaxed, waspish under pressure . . . friendly,

THE WINNINGEST CHAMP

Dick Johnson of Dallas, Texas, has won more U.S. National Soaring Championships than any other pilot; his victories span a quarter of a century. He is virtually a permanent member of the U.S. Team in international competition. Deadly consistency is his trademark; he rarely errs, and has a knack of making good days out of crummy ones.

outgoing and open with newcomers to the sport . . .
impatient to the point of rapid anger with those who
violate his personal code in the air (*i.e.*, chasing him from
thermal to thermal like a school of mullet). . . critical of
modern contest philosophy, which he accuses of pampering
high-performance bombs at the expense of "average" ships
("The bombs only like to fly on booming days, so the
officials cancel us out when the weather is marginal.") . . .
His flying is always marked by chronometer precision, self-
discipline, and freedom from errors; his consistency is
deadly, to the continuing frustration of younger hotshots
who wishfully think him over the hill. No way.

Darkly tanned, lean, quick-witted, our close friend Ben
Greene is rapid of speech for a Southerner, but the Tar
Heel twang is unmistakable in person or on the contest
frequency . . . tautly tuned for every competition, yet
enjoys relaxed banter on the grid until just before launch-
ing . . . then he slips on his soft, black competition gloves
and becomes very businesslike indeed . . . Complete master
of every plane he flies, but never ever showy . . . Knowing
pilots fight for the privilege of buying an ex-Ben Greene
sailplane, for it has been more finely competition-tuned
than anything else around . . . One of the Quiet Birdmen
during most tasks, but he can be heard relaying radio
messages for downed pilots toward the end of each day . . .
An impeccable dresser, he can afford the best of everything, yet his unfailing courtesy, warmth and sportsmanship
endear him to the peasantry . . . If there is a soaring
aristocracy, Ben is the Prince. A day spent with men like
these goes so quickly; too quickly.

By the morning of July 9th, the front had finally passed,
but a claggy residue of altocumulus stubbornly clung to the
Bryan area. Undaunted, the task committee called for an
optimistic Speed Triangle, with turnpoints at Charlotte

(charLOTTE in Michiganese) and Three Rivers; distance, 202 miles.

By twilight, there were twelve finishers; Dick Johnson's winning speed was a dignified 35.5 mph. And that sums up the day. Perhaps in deference to the non-finishers, none of The Magnificent Dozen claimed an easy flight. In fact, planes had begun plopping to earth less than Silver C distance[3] from the start gate that afternoon. They continued to litter the countryside along the remaining legs, yet many managed to struggle at least as far as Three Rivers. Aside from Johnson, most of the front-runners went down somewhere along the third leg; glory was reserved for the floaters, many of whom arrived quite late at Three Rivers where they encountered the first sunshine anyone had seen in hours. Conditions quickly recycled, and they were able to climb out for a very delicate ride home at maximum L/D.[4]

Again the scores were turned upside down, including the top level; those who had foolishly written off Dick Johnson as a has-been took a surprised look at the preliminary figures that night. In both the daily and cumulative columns, Johnson's name led all the rest!

By July 10th, the lethargic cold front had gone stationary south of Bryan; the frontal showers were sending greetings back north in the form of a thick overcast that lurked over the contest site throughout the day. The only possible task, Prescribed Area Distance,[5] was duly

---

[3] Silver C distance: 50 kilometers, or 31.1 statute miles. The reference is to the F.A.I. Soaring Badge program, which progresses from the Silver C through the Gold Badge to the Gold Badge with Diamonds.

[4] L/D: Lift-Drag ratio, or glide angle, usually expressed as (for example) 40:1, which means that in still air, at a certain airspeed, the glider will travel 40 feet forward for every foot of altitude used. The airspeed that gives maximum L/D is relatively slow: 50-60 knots for most modern sailplanes.

[5] Prescribed Area Distance: a variation on the old Free-Distance task, in which pilots fly to any of the designated turnpoints they choose, the pilot covering the greatest distance being the winner. For a more detailed description, see page (48).

announced, to the predictable groans of pilots and crews alike.

A number of brave hearts were towed off at their pre-selected launch times; most were back on the airport at Bryan within 30 minutes, while a few glided straight into the boonies 8 to 12 miles out. When Paul Bikle and Stan Smith both returned for relights,[6] there was a stampede to the Start Board to select later launch times; both of these oldtimers are famous for hanging on when the entire sky is falling.

After 1300, another surge of launches, but a majority of pilots had tugged their planes to the side of the runway with the notion that things couldn't possibly get worse, so why not wait until they got better? By now the lively game of Start Board Roulette was so absorbing that those of us still delaying our tows failed to notice that there were practically no relights from that second batch of launches. It was to prove a costly oversight.

For it was the second group which included nearly all of the 18 pilots who exceeded 100 miles distance for the day, and earned themselves appropriate scores. Tiptoeing north, scraping away at every vestige of vagrant lift, they gradually inched toward the beckoning sunlight and towering cu's[7] some 30 to 40 miles north of Bryan. (We who remained on the ground, clustered around the start board, had been watching those cu's; but we could not conceive of any way to reach them from a 2000-foot tow.)

Those who struggled out from under the overcast ran into just the jolly soaring conditions Chuck Lindsay had prophesied: narrow but strong bands of lift beneath streets of cu's, interspersed with dead, blue areas.

A. J. Smith, upon whom meteorological signposts are

[6]relight: another launch.

[7]cu's: cumulus clouds, which are always formed by rising air, and therefore helpful signposts to lift.

never wasted, was once more back in the saddle. Taking utmost advantage of every working cloud in the big open semicircle north, northwest and northeast of Bryan, he brought home enough turnpoint pictures to total 214.5 miles after a day of astonishing success against dreadful odds.

Meanwhile, back at the contest site, Elemer Katinsky and Ed Byars had worked up a list of groundcrews known to have left the airport (denoting pilots who were presumably covering distance somewhere out in the Prescribed Area.) To make it an official contest day, 15 pilots must exceed 60 miles; after eliminating all departees who were positively known to be down, there were 16 names left—all potentially alive and well and with more than 60 miles under their wings. This precipitated another wild scramble to the start board, and a flurry of by-now late afternoon tows; suddenly we were confronted with the ugly possibility of scoring zero for the day.

At 1800, there were weak thermals around Bryan, and huge gaggles began working them up to 2500 AGL[8]. Topping out, one by one the ships slipped off into the gathering twilight, some heading south, others north. For most, it was a smooth final glide to a pasture or a chance airport ten or 15 miles away. A few found another patch of lift or so, and eked out 20- to 30-mile rides. I drove north for about nine miles in totally dead air, weighing the risks of an off-field landing against the desirability of having a healthy ship for the next day's battle (a very few points *vs.* a possibly nasty groundloop in the high crops below). With a sigh, I reluctantly turned 180° and floated back to Bryan to collect my well-deserved zero for the day. It was not one of my big moments.

[8] AGL: Above Ground Level, or the actual height above the terrain. MSL: Mean Sea Level, which denotes absolute altitude without reference to the local terrain. Usually we refer to AGL when working at lower altitudes, where every foot counts.

Dick Johnson took second place for the day with a Gold-distance flight of 186.5 miles, further tightening his grip on second overall. Ben Greene was fourth for the day, but now trailed Johnson by more than 300 points.

Driving toward Williams County Airport at 4:30 a.m., July 11th, Chuck Lindsay splashed through a steady, heavy downpour. It certainly looked like another rest day, but after checking all the available data, the Incurable Optimist (Ben Greene's affectionate phrase) began to see possibilities of a soarable day to the northwest. Thus a short Speed Triangle was hatched: turnpoints at Coldwater and Marshall, Michigan; distance, 124.5 miles.

The glop overhead seemed reluctant to leave; the first launch didn't clear the field until 1336. It quickly became apparent the weather wasn't cooperating out in the task area, either, when ominous numbers of the early birds came straggling back to Bryan for relights.

Big gaggles were forming out on the first leg wherever the lift exceeded 100 fpm. There were cu's along the way, but many of them proved useless, and the lift beneath others was weak, narrow and shifty. A brisk, quartering headwind was also getting in its evil licks. Eventually the gaggles dwindled as various pilots began pursuing their own inspirations.

Early on, I had the cheery experience of leading an impressive gaggle from thermal to thermal, always out front and on top and feeling rather like Teddy Roosevelt at San Juan Hill. Someday I must engrave and mount on my panel the homily: "Pride goeth before a fall." From my position of some slight advantage, I promptly flew myself into a scrape, suffered the ignominy of having Dick Johnson (quite unaware) dump his ballast all over me, and lost a fateful 30 minutes scratching for dear life near one of those 1,000 Michigan lakes full of misbegotten, happy sailboaters. By this time, I had fallen far behind the main body of adventurers, and it looked as though I was about three thermals away from any visible source of lift.

Perhaps someday Chuck Lindsay will take me on his knee and explain how it is possible to glide for miles and miles through sink that averages 4-500 fpm down, with sparsely scattered thermals that average 1-200 fpm up. Doesn't all that sinking air create unbearable pressures at ground level? Do people run around like crazy down there, holding their ears and shrieking with pain?

I found myself racing around the sky, shrieking with frustration. After an interminable climb back to "safe" altitude, in short order I snapped my pictures at Coldwater and pressed on directly upwind toward Marshall; in still shorter order, I blew nearly 5000 feet of hard-won altitude, trying to fight that tigerish sink with kittenish thermals. Four times in half-an-hour, I had the gear down for landing. High up and far ahead, I caught tantalizing glimpses of a vast gaggle, as I clawed and grasped at every devious bubble kicked up by the surface turbulence.

I was beginning to see clearly why soaring is one of the world's least popular sports when, in the midst of a resigned final glide toward the runway at Marshall, I caught an encouraging bump and at long last whirled into something fit for climbing. Soaring, I decided back at 2500 AGL, has its moments after all.

There are few pleasures in the air that can top photographing a turnpoint from safe altitude—especially a turnpoint you never really expected to see, let alone reach. For about ten seconds, I savored this small triumph, then reverted to worrying about my next thermal while I let the wind at last do something constructive, like helping me go home. In less than ten minutes, my worries were over. I had landed safely in the parking area of a motorcycle speedway, less than a dozen miles from Marshall.

After calling contest headquarters to bare my shame and galvanize my crew, I raced back to save my plane from a horde of beer-drinking bike-fans and their filthy urchins. Perhaps some of my cautionary remarks were intemperate; shortly there was a drunken Lufbery Circle of motorbikes weaving perilously close to Tango Tango's defenseless wings.

Under different circumstances, I might have smiled tolerantly. But I had just finished the fifth in a series of fiascos worse than any I had ever contrived to string together in competition. A Gothic black rage boiled up inside me, and before I knew what I was doing, I had grabbed one of the cycles by the handlebars, somehow stalling its motor, and was growling into the miscreant's blurry face: "Come near my plane one more time, Buddy, and I'll tear your (bleep) bike apart with my bare hands!" I was then left in peace until my crew arrived.

Objectivity did not return that night. Straggling into Contest HQ at a late hour and learning that 40 pilots had completed the day's triangle served only to deepen my depression. A. J. Smith had again led the pack with a speed of 49.1 mph. Big deal. Jim Smiley had put together one of his flawless, beautiful flights and soared back into the Top Ten with a second-place finish at 44.6 mph. Wowee and so forth. Ben Greene was a close third at 44.4 mph (one or two claps). Dick Johnson, sixth for the day, had the cumulative points to remain firmly entrenched in second overall. I couldn't have cared less.

Driving south toward Bryan earlier that night, I had felt an overpowering temptation to go straight on through and keep driving until we were back home in South Carolina. By now, I *hated* this contest. But from the seat beside me came silent waves of understanding and tactfully tacit encouragement; with Trudy along, quitting was out of the question.

That night, I dropped down to 49th: the backside of the scoresheet.

Throughout the contest, we Southern troops had been faring worse at Bryan than our granddaddies did at Gettysburg. Finally, on the 6th contest day (July 12), the South rose up in all its antebellum glory and smote the Yankee hosts hip and thigh.

In his booming parade-ground voice, Bob Jackson announced the day's exercise: a moderate Speed Triangle, using the airports at Lima and Bowling Green as turnpoints; distance, 154.5 miles.

Thanks entirely to a very early start, I saw only one or two other ships at work along the first leg, then no one else for the rest of the flight. After crossing the finish line and pulling up perhaps a bit more steeply than strictly necessary (it had been a while since my last finish), I looked down incredulously at the contest site: there wasn't a single sailplane on the ground! At least, I reflected happily, none of the later starters had lapped me!

(A few moments earlier, gunning for the finish line, I had called in the regulation "Tango Tango, two miles out!" I quite expected the gate to come back with a startled *"Who?"*—but they were gentlemen about it, acting as if my star-crossed ship had been among the early finishers every day.)

Nearly everyone had found it necessary to deviate from the strict courseline that day, especially on the second and third legs. There were occasional cu's some miles southeast of the track between Lima and Bowling Green which were well worth the extra miles involved; on-course, there was mostly chop.

From Bowling Green west back to Bryan, we had to run above the Maumee River valley. The air over the valley looked dead as a hammer, and it was; it deserved a simple funeral, right then and there; no flowers, please. My trusty

Polaroid shades disclosed some milky wisps punching through the inversion north of course, though, and once I reached these my troubles were over.

Ben Greene had his best flight of the contest, too, despite some bad moments near the village of Napoleon (a scant 20 miles from the finish line); he recovered in time to earn 1000 points for the day. Jim Smiley, the Racin' Rebel, came in second. A. J. Smith protected his huge lead by placing a good third. And turning to the back page of the daily scoresheet, we find Gren Seibels was fourth.

And just how, you wonder, does A. J. Smith fit in with all those Suth'n boys? All together, students:

BECAUSE HE'S FROM *SOUTH*FIELD, MICHIGAN.

While the Dixielanders were having a great day, Chuck Forrester was having a wretched one. Shot down soon after his first tow, he couldn't quite make it back to Williams County airport, and had to squeeze into a small emergency patch a half-mile to the west. Retrieved, reassembled and airborne again, he soon came to grief out on course, couldn't recover, and again was forced to land—this time in a vast open field that portended no problems at all. Yet as he touched down, his *Libelle* went into a violent ground-loop, breaking the fuselage in half.

A farmer was placidly mowing hay in the adjoining field. Before, during and after the accident, he kept right on mowing imperturbably. Only after Chuck's crew had stowed the bits and pieces in the trailer did the farmer halt his mowing and amble over to ask questions. Chuck inquired about his delayed-reaction curiosity.

"I didn't want to come over here," explained the farmer matter-of-factly, "until they got the body out."

At the pilots' meeting next day, A. J. went over his tactics for the previous day and revealed his prescription for dealing with erratic, disorganized lift. "There were some stretches where effective circling was difficult," he reported, "so when I couldn't thermal"—here a porpoising-upwards motion with his hand—"I just climbed straight ahead!"

A whingdilly of a cold front was now passing through the area, with winds gusting to 40 knots, so another no-contest day was declared. My loyal crew maintained the pleasant fiction that I was the fourth-best soaring pilot in the U. S. for 48 enchanting hours.

July 14th, Bastille Day in France, and the penultimate contest day for 60-odd soaring pilots at Bryan, provided the ultimate in both weather and task. In the wake of the previous day's bustling cold front, classic soaring conditions were forecast—and delivered. The only insect in the soup was a persistent northwest wind aloft, of some 25-30 knots velocity at cruising altitudes. So when Bob Jackson announced the day's Speed Triangle, with turnpoints at Tiffin, Ohio, and Charlotte, Michigan, with total distance of 281.5 miles, there was a great rustling of charts, followed by long, low whistles as we realized the lengthy second leg (131 miles) would be right into the teeth of those winds.

By way of compensation, lift was expected to average 4-500 fpm by noon, occasionally 600 fpm later on, with cloudbases at 7000 MSL. The thing sounded feasible, but it looked like a long day in the saddle.

A few quick statistics tell the main story: all but 13 of the starters completed the triangle, really a big one by Eastern standards; total mileage flown for the day was just shy of 15,000!

By dusk, A. J. Smith had stretched his record to five wins in seven days. If it sounds too easy, here's his story:

"Our biggest problem was getting started . . . we didn't have a car yet. (A. J.'s silver Pontiac had expired in mid-contest.) Lew Lemley came through with a car about 10 a.m. and we made numerous trips into town to get our equipment and our ship put together. We never did really make it. You probably noticed me parked at the side of the takeoff line. After the last sailplane had left, we got out on the runway and got a very slow tow—really frustrating—the guy was flying at about 70 to 75 knots and climbing at about 50 feet a minute. He took me out by Montpelier and around through all the down areas.

"Ben and I started about the same time. I began immediately to prepare my maps and courses; I spent most of the first leg drawing the course lines, and trying to get the maps folded—a real task in the AS-W 12 cockpit . . . I made the turnpoint, got pretty low—and low to me is 1500 feet—and got back up on course about ten miles out as a lot of you did. It was difficult and slow to get back up again. I did it mostly by trying to figure out where the blasted streets were and then climbing straight ahead." (There, he said it again!)

"I got up about east of Bowling Green and from that point on things went pretty well, except that I thought I would finally have time for some breakfast. I opened a can of Sego and I immediately had Sego on the canopy and down the front of my shirt. I got about two swallows, and it was pretty turbulent, and I decided it was a bad deal. You can't let loose of a stick in the 12, so if you can imagine opening a can of Sego and trying to drink it and keep your hand on top of it at the same time, it's quite a job.

"I finally threw the thing out and immediately got Sego all over the airplane. Then I spent the rest of the leg literally cleaning Sego out of the inside of the cockpit. It was getting pretty sticky.

"I worked thermals fairly regularly, I suppose every ten miles or so, and they were good thermals. I was getting achieved rates of climb of 450-475 fpm, and I cruised off

**WHEN I COULDN'T THERMAL,
I JUST CLIMBED STRAIGHT AHEAD!**

A. J. Smith describes his new speed tactic to a pilots' meeting, later dubbed "porpoising" after the rest of us caught on. Victory at Bryan was another high-water mark in his brilliant soaring career.

the first 1000 or 2000 feet at about 100 knots to get out
of the higher headwinds, and then slowed down to 85
knots. The gaggles were able to stay with me pretty well
for about ten to twelve miles.

"I ended up south of Albion and I came into the
turnpoint (Charlotte) a little bit from the southwest
because there was a string of clouds to the west of it. I was
staying about one row of clouds in from the edge of a blue
hole, and I had a feeling as I went out into the blue hole
that it might have been better right at the edge of the hole
because I had a couple of really good thermals there—they
seemed to be better formed and a little bit stronger.

"Then the turnpoint and back out again without too
much trouble. I had to come back out almost straight
south and a little southwest again to get the shortest
distance to the clouds. Again I think that was probably not
necessary, because I hit a couple of little spots of lift in the
clear blue, and from that point on it was pretty much
flying the streets."

First leg fussing with charts, second leg doing the breakfast dishes—and still he outflew the whole crowd.

Very late that afternoon, pilots and crews were lingering
in the tie-down area, hashing over the day's adventures,
when someone spotted a big *Cirrus* floating in, low and
slow, from the northwest. It was Dr. Ernst Steinhoff's
3-Lima, and there was a bare chance that a straight-in
landing and a long roll-out might get him across the finish
line at mid-runway.

We began cheering as he slowly closed the distance, for
now he seemed to have it in the bag; then the cheers froze
as we saw his drag-chute deploy just before he touched
down. Someone with a big heart got on the radio and
shouted: "Dr. Steinhoff, jettison your chute!"

By now, the big ship was barely crawling toward the

checkered yellow flags marking the finish line. Obediently, the chute fell away from 3-Lima's tail, and the *Cirrus* crept on toward the two flags until its nosecone was perhaps six inches over the magic line; a wing dropped, and for a moment all was quiet. Then the cheers broke out again.

The intrepid old German had finished!

Overheard late one afternoon:

Knowledgeable spectator to pilot, who has just landed with water still dripping from his undercarriage: "Did you carry water all the way around?"

Pilot: "Hell no, that's sweat!"

Despite his sticky bout with the Sego can the day before, A. J. Smith turned up at the final pilots' briefing looking about as worried as a cat choking on whipping cream. He had a fat 460-point lead going into the stretch, achieved through a brilliant string of flights against the toughest competition in the country.

Following the Long Triangle of the 14th, during which some pilots had logged seven to eight hours in their cockpits, announcement that the final task would be another Prescribed Area Distance was met with the most restrained enthusiasm imaginable.

But Chuck Lindsay's sketch of the mixed bag of weather conditions around the envelope tended to validate the Task Committee's decision. Subsequent flying experience confirmed the choice as a wise one.

As launch time neared, the sky looked better than it actually was. Cu's were slowly forming in the vicinity of Bryan, and between high belts of cirrus and altocumulus, the sun was hot and bright. A fairly stiff breeze from the west suggested a downwind drift toward eastern turnpoints to some pilots; others decided to work crosswind toward one of the southern goals, and play it by ear from there. A

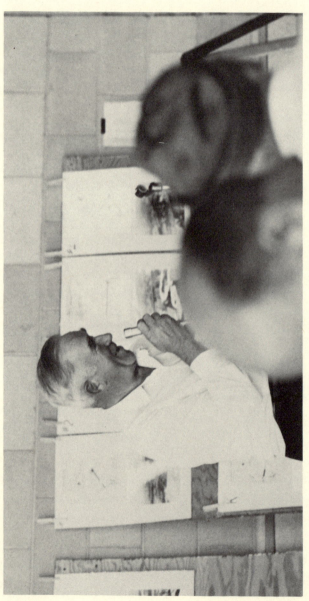

HE MADE IT!

Dr. Ernst Steinhoff, one of the pioneer German soaring pilots before World War II, remained active in U.S. competition until well into the 1970s. Here he tells a pilots' meeting about his squeaky finish at Bryan.

few independents (including Dick Johnson) elected to fight the headwinds at the outset, aiming southwest. The entire northwest quadrant was blocked with a thick cirrus blanket.

(It was, in point of fact, a classic Cat's Cradle situation, demanding careful analysis and continuous decision-making by every pilot, from pre-flight planning through the entire afternoon until the moment of landing. Some of the best flights resulted from completely different tactics, wherein lies some of the fascination of the task.

(These thoughts flow from mellow hindsight; at the time, I was far too weary for philosophy.)

Crossing the town of Bryan on tow, I felt a powerful surge of lift and released into a fat, strong thermal that took me to 5000 in jigtime. I quickly dispatched my crew south toward Richmond, Indiana—in line with my preflight strategy of working crosswind—and following the green checkerboard of section lines below, I went bucketing southward myself. There ensued a long hour of frustration as I chased one cu after another, only to find that 90-percent of them were dead or dying. Only after a hair-raising save near Van Wert did it dawn on me that the boomer over Bryan was a fluke; this was going to be a hard day's work. I instructed myself to forget about the dishonest cu's, and concentrate instead on the scattered patches of sunlight moving eastward across the fields below; sometimes the surface warmed enough to send up a half-hearted little thermal.

My poor crew! I kept them backing and filling for six hours that day, as one turnpoint after another receded from the realm of possibility. During most of the flight, thoughts of speed and distance had to be set aside; merely staying in the air required my full attention.

After abandoning Richmond (which Ben and several others managed to reach—I never found out how), I spent about three hours scratching my way to Sidney, Ohio—

really a series of final glides with an unlikely save near the end of each. At one low point I got a midair drenching from Hannes Linke, who elected to dump his ballast moments after I had decided that his miserable thermal was less miserable than my miserable thermal, and moved in below him. Surviving this indignity, I had the evil pleasure of outclimbing him near the top of the thermal—but alas, my own ballast had long since gone, so I could only repay him with a sweet smile as I gazed down into his cockpit.

In view of the blood, sweat and tears expended in order to reach Sidney, I felt I had earned the luxury of a downwind drift, so the crew and I pointed ourselves toward Marion, the first turnpoint northeast of Sidney. Sternly I counseled myself to work every scrap of lift while letting the wind do the cross-country part of the job. Sound advice, assuming there was any lift; there was none.

The final-glide-and-save sequence was still in vogue, but as I watched the town of Bellefontaine ominously climbing up my canopy, I began to have doubts about executing the "save" part of the formula. Cycling the gear down (for perhaps the sixth time that day), I circled the handsome little airport north of town, my car and trailer in sharp view as they parked by the hangar and patiently awaited developments. Utterly exhausted, mentally and physically, I realized I was looking forward to the release of an honorable landing; how I craved to stretch my legs, inhale a cool beer, and call it a contest!

I found myself automatically banking into a bump at about 200 feet. Giving it a careless circle or two, fervently hoping it would disappear like all the others, I found instead that I was climbing back out at a zippy 150 fpm. Sigh. "Squaredance,[9] move out toward Marion. SLOWLY!"

[9]Squaredance: My personal radio call for my ground crew; a reference to my sailplane's competition identification, Tango Tango. When Ben Greene was flying "Gooney Bird," his crew responded to "Nest." Strict constructionists

Nearing Marion, low as always, I finally spotted what I'd been praying for all day: a fat row of black-bottomed, billowing cumulus in a long east-west line. Just under the edge of these lovely monsters, I swung into the best thermal of the day: nearly 500 fpm on the averager. As we spiraled upwards, Tango Tango and I, the sour, aching weariness magically lifted; each turn of the altimeter needle was like a gentle massage. At 6000, feeling like a brand new man, I watched the ground below fog out, and broke away for turnpoint photos.

Hungry now for some more of this type of action, I decided to continue the northeastward drift to Norwalk; but en route, as I approached Bucyrus, I began to see what the haze had obscured: those big, black clouds over Norwalk had huge anvil tops; now I could see the lightning flashes below.

Okay, let's try Toledo. Hmmm—looks a mite bleak up that way; better call them for a weather advisory. I tuned the tower frequency, but before I could start talking, I intercepted Toledo Radio's reply to some other pilots: " . . . had a big thunderstorm through here . . . we now have 600 scattered, 1200 broken and 6000 overcast. Surface winds are calm . . . "

"Squaredance, go to Upper Sandusky *fast*, and head west *slow*!" If I could just sneak back under that ever-loving east-west line of cumulus I'd already used near Marion— now many miles to the south—I could make a glorious run back toward Bryan. If . . .

It was a long, long glide with not a ripple in the air to suggest that I was airborne. The variometers for the next 15 minutes glued themselves to 1 1/2 knots down, as we fought a losing race between altitude and distance. By the

frown on these games, but I could never call Trudy "Tango Tango Ground" with a straight face.

time I reached the downwind side of those still-towering cu's, I was well below 1000. Instead of the hoped-for lift, I barged into sink that grew worse the farther I penetrated beneath the vast clouds.

By dint of brilliant driving, the crew and I had once more converged; while I followed a buzzard (who was also vainly searching for lift), Trudy inspected the plowed field below and advised a gear-up landing. I jounced and skidded to a stop 50 feet from where she stood.

Since turning Marion, I had done a bunch of flying, but all of it in a big semi-circle as I kept changing goals. My net distance for scoring after more than six hours of desperate flying was an unimpressive 175 miles. There were several of us tied at 29th that day, yet I managed to keep my precarious hold on the front side of the scoresheet!

Meanwhile, on a very different level, more important issues were being decided.

With 231.5 miles and sixth place for the day, A. J. Smith had clinched the U. S. National Soaring Championship—his third. His cumulative score of 7485 stood only 515 points short of 8000-point perfection.

The real cliff-hanger of the day was the Johnson-Greene tilt for overall second spot. Just before dark, Ben called in to report a 248-mile flight, the best of the day—so far. Had he done it? Had he finally overtaken Johnson with the magic 89 points?

But Johnson had not yet called in. Nine o'clock, nine-thirty, ten o'clock; many exhausted pilots gave up the vigil and went home to sleep. Still no word from Johnson.

At long last, the contest phone rang: Dick Johnson, reporting 261 miles and a difficult retrieve! His 1000 points for the final day settled it: he had wound up 138 points ahead of Greene, and only 347 points behind A. J.

I'm not speaking for the winner, obviously, nor for the runners-up; but for the also-rans, the letdown after a major

contest is overpowering. For the better part of a year, we
have been fettling, practicing, psyching ourselves up for the
Big One. To each major contest, we bring a high-strung
and complex package of taut nerves, timid hopes, semi-
suppressed fears, and enough internal adrenalin to wet
down the whole runway. Day after day, we struggle to do
the Competition Director's bidding—do it better than everyone else; yet—grinding around in a wretched thermal after a
heart-stopping save, we chance to look up and catch the
glint of high wings serenely cruising thousands of feet
above us, and taste the bitter self-knowledge that, after all,
we just aren't really good enough to win.

But the next day dawns with the challenge of a new
task, and we cling to the chance that in our string of
disasters this one day may shine brightly, brilliantly, on our
endeavors. And it does happen, just often enough to keep
us from chucking the whole business and rejoining church
and country club.

Then one morning we pop awake—a ten-day old habit—
and our first thought is, *Thank God, no task today*! Quick
on its heels comes the second thought, *No more chances to
catch up; it's over, damn it*!

For the losers, breakfast is quiet, although we assemble
our best smile for other pilots and their crews at adjoining
tables. Later, we are drawn irresistibly back to the airfield,
where we find many other pilots wandering aimlessly,
bemused and abstracted. The skies overhead swarm with
white competition ships as crewchiefs enjoy "gratitude"
rides aboard their pilots' planes. Winds are light; hardwork-
ing cu's stretch across the sky in all directions; visibility is
unlimited; it's a go-anywhere soaring day. Trudy and I
savor a charming hour together in the Bryan Soaring Club's
Ka-7, effortlessly wafting to cloudbase again and again; an
ironic contrast with most of the preceding days, when such
things might have counted.

Back on the ground, we make desultory small-talk with old friends and new acquaintances ... all of us, I think, sharing a nagging sensation that we have forgotten something important: we should *be* somewhere, right this minute, *doing* something! But until the banquet, there's really nothing to do. *Drop by our room for a drink, why don't you?* Okay, fine, what time? *Why not right now?*

What seems the longest day of all finally slopes into evening, and we welcome the banquet hour—at last, something concrete to do. It is hot in the packed dining room, but the speeches are mercifully brief, the jokes are passable—and I notice that through it all, A. J. smiles ... and smiles ... and smiles.

3

HINDSIGHT

It is said that when someone once asked an old hand to name the biggest danger in soaring, he thought for a moment, and said: "Starvation."

Although the story is probably apocryphal, the point is sound; given any sort of lift, a modern sailplane in the hands of a competent pilot can stay up indefinitely. Kidneys and sore butts cause more landings than gravity. I never get hungry while flying, but I often construct a searing thirst; if the anecdote had been about me, the answer would have been "dehydration." A few close saves will do it every time.

Spoiled as we are today, with our high performance ships and the shared secrets of several generations of flyers, we find it hard to believe that a scant 50 years ago, the five-minute duration flight was still just a dream for most glider pilots. Orville Wright, who *loved* gliding, was still fooling around with motorless flight in 1911 when he soared the dunes at Kitty Hawk for just over nine minutes, a world record that would stand for the next decade. Not until the early 1920s did a few of the German soaring pioneers figure out ways to improve on Orville's achievement; in this country, the record stood until 1929. Yet when you consider the primitive machinery they were using, and the fact that no one had discovered thermals, it's not terribly surprising that some of those tireless enthusiasts needed upwards of a hundred bungee launches to log an hour's gliding time.

It has been pointed out that the ancient Egyptians

41

certainly had the technology and the materials necessary to build an airworthy glider; all they lacked was the idea. You can waste some fascinating hours speculating on what the course of history might have been, had an Otto Lilienthal or a John Montgomery come into the world during the reign of Tut-Ankh-Amen. Yet, thousands of years later, the very brightest light of the Renaissance—Leonardo da Vinci—still missed the basic point. Studying sparrows instead of eagles, he wasted his formidable talent designing machines to flap instead of soar.

We were well into the 19th century before the fixed-wing (or fixed-plane) concept began to be taken seriously, and from then on, controlled human flight was no longer a question of if, but when. (Ballooning is flying, of course, but since it's about 98-percent uncontrolled, let's skip it here.) For fifty years, a succession of brave and brilliant men wrestled with the awesome riddles of stability, lift, drag and other unfamiliar forces until the Wrights finally put it all together and led the world into the sky.

Whatever they knew about flying they learned from gliders; yet after the pivotal moment of that first powered flight at Kitty Hawk, gliders ironically became the first casualties of the aeronautical evolution they had made possible. The world suddenly went bananas over aviation—powered aviation—which arrived on the scene just in time to provide the sole grace-note of romance amidst the butchery of World War I. In point of fact, the colorful *escadrilles* and *jagdstaffeln* had precious little strategic impact on the outcome of those ghastly hostilities, but their wild adventures high above the trenches fired everyone's imagination, opening the way for the coming Air Age.

Had it not been for the vindictiveness, understandable but naive, of the framers of the Versailles Treaty, the sport of soaring might indeed have been buried in the sands at Kitty Hawk. In 1919, the victorious allies were obsessed with schemes to cripple once and for all Germany's capacity to wage war. Among other strictures, the Germans were forbidden to resume manufacture of conventional aircraft. Thus gliders became the only legal option for German pilots hoping to revive sport flying in the conquered nation. While Europe licked her wounds, the sport of soaring came back to life on the slopes of the Wasserküppe in 1920.

For most of the ensuing decade, the Germans had it pretty much to themselves. Bungee-launching off the high Bavarian pastures into the steady slope winds, they taught themselves the art of ridge-soaring, and soon began setting records for duration and even distance as they prowled along the winding mountainsides. As new techniques evolved, so did sailplane technology; toward the end of the '20s, there began to appear some extraordinarily beautiful gullwing designs, tapered planforms of high aspect ratio attached to carefully streamlined fuselages. Aboard these graceful craft, pilots found they could maintain and even gain altitude in the gentlest ridge-lift.

In 1928, a group of the German pilots visited this country, bringing their ships so they could stage soaring demonstrations for the handful of American enthusiasts who would go on to form the nucleus of the soaring movement in the United States. By 1930, these native pioneers felt they were ready to mount the first U. S. National Soaring Championships at Elmira, New York. According to Ralph Barnaby (who, of course, was there), it was during this contest that the German, Wolf Hirth, took a late afternoon launch when the air was too calm for ridge-lift—and made an extended soaring flight! Hirth had stumbled onto thermal soaring, and he had the intelligence to grasp the implications. You can date modern soaring from that chance flight over Chemung County in upstate New York in the summer of 1930.

For the next several years, however, the sport clung to
the ridges. In nearly every major mountain system in the
world, there are certain seasons when prevailing winds can
be depended upon, night and day, to produce ridge-lift.
This fact was not lost on soaring pilots, who plunged into
enthusiastic, if witless, competition for new endurance
records. Once past the 24-hour mark, these exercises proved
little beyond a pilot's ability to stave off sleep. After a
scandalous number of exhausted flyers had nodded at their
controls, frequently with fatal results, the F. A. I.[1] finally
scrubbed duration flights from the official records,
removing the incentive for further suicidal heroics. Students
of human folly will note that the fad for flagpole sitting
waxed and waned in the same era.

Besides, more challenging and instructive adventures were
at hand. By now, the Germans had proceeded far enough
with the theory of thermal flight to develop primitive but
functioning variometers; at long last they were released
from bondage to the hills, free to soar wherever the sun
shone. Some remarkable cross-country flights ensued,
including several for Diamond Distance (500 kilometers).
The sport became inherently safer once it broke away from
the heavily forested mountain slopes and moved out over
the open countryside, where landable fields abounded.

But safety is not every man's goal. Some of the more
intrepid Germans invented the game of aerial chicken,
pursuing thermals up into building cu's, competing to see
who could climb farthest before getting into trouble. Since
they flew without gyro attitude instruments, the game
required abundant quantities of skill, guts and luck to
survive unscathed. Severe icing claimed several victims, but
most of the losers predictably became disoriented and

---

[1]F.A.I.: Federation Aeronautique Internationale, official rule-making and
record-keeping body for all competitive aviation around the world, with headquarters in Paris.

wound up in the nemesis of all blind flying, the spiral dive. Hauling back on the stick with might and main to slow the terrifying airspeed, they simply steepened the angle of bank and added to the stresses on the airframe until everything let go. The lucky ones parachuted safely to earth.

One feckless chap reportedly bored into the bottom of an enormous cumulonimbus and was climbing at an incredible rate when his ship blundered into such powerful turbulence it disintegrated around him. He separated himself from the remains and opened his parachute. Of course it was bitterly cold, but he knew this would moderate as he descended through the storm cloud. Some moments later he realized it was growing still colder. Then he understood with terrible finality what was happening: somehow he had drifted back into the enormous lifting core of the storm and was being swept higher and higher. It is not known whether he died of hypoxia, or simply froze to death; when the storm eventually released his corpse, it floated gently to earth many miles from the wreckage of his ship.

When soaring was abandoned by the technician-inventors and subsequently taken over by sportsmen, it inevitably became a competitive game. Gaggles of enthusiasts, without a death-wish among them, began gathering each summer on the mountain meadows of Bavaria with their homebuilt sailplanes, each an original design, to show their stuff. They competed in such matters as duration, distance, and altitude gains, and as word of their prowess began to circulate in other countries, a few amateurs in England and elsewhere commenced dabbling in the sport. But by now the Germans were so far out front in design, technique and experience they utterly dominated the field until World War II. What's more, German sailplanes have continued to be the ships to beat in international competition to this day.

The misuse of gliders by both sides during World War II borders on the criminal, and fills the sorriest chapter in the history of motorless flight. Apparently no one in command on either side had the faintest understanding of a glider's potential, and what was worse, of its limitations. The consequence was the witless sacrifice of legions of brave young men in doomed night landings over terrain studded with tank traps or natural barriers, or tow-releases over open seas, miles short of designated drop-points. Students of military ineptitude can point to similar waste and tragedy throughout the course of history, but in this case, the whole concept of powerless flight fell under a dark shadow it didn't really deserve. Had such wicked stupidity prevailed among the various fighter and bomber commands, the development of commercial and general aviation in the postwar years would have been severely stunted. As it is, to this day many who remember the disasters that befell military gliders 30-odd years ago consider the sport of soaring a game for fools impatient to greet Eternity. Never mind catechizing the enormous difference between attempting to survive a crash-landing in an overloaded troop-carrier in pitch-black darkness on unknown terrain, and the use we make of the modern competition sailplane; their minds were closed and locked in the early '40s.

Despite all this, however, the sport soon revived following the war. Surplus trainers dominated the entry-lists in American competition during the immediate postwar years. Toward the end of the decade, a trickle of new designs began to appear—notably the landmark 1-23 from the Schweizer factory in Elmira, and a few years later, from Germany, Schleicher's wonderful Ka-6, soon followed by the Schempp-Hirth *Austria*. In those days, contest points were still being awarded for altitude gains; free-distance tasks were in vogue, since rarely did anyone cover more than a hundred miles or so. Contest rules were simple and informal, administration was lax to the point of slap-dash, and a good time was reportedly enjoyed by all.

It is said that a pilot could win a National contest during this period simply by the avoidance of serious blunders—implying that during the normal course of events, everyone else would sooner or later goof. Entry qualifications of the day were not very stringent: if you had a license and a sailplane, you were welcome. To phrase it politely, the average level of pilot performance then was, well, mediocre.

Then, in the mid-1960s, the quiet, steady evolution of sailplane technology and soaring technique began leaping ahead with bewildering speed; the evolution became a near-revolution. In this country, the expanding program of SSA[2]-sanctioned Regionals began training bumper crops of shrewd, skillful and highly competition-oriented pilots, while simultaneously, in Germany, an aeronautical wizard and his wife were lovingly creating the prototype of the first all-fiberglass production sailplane—in their kitchen. From glass cloth, balsa and epoxy, Eugen and Ursula Hänle fashioned their remarkable 15-meter H-301 *Libelle*, in both design and structure years ahead of anything then flying.

Almost overnight, Herr Hänle's achievement was recognized by the German industry as the end of the road for traditional aluminum or wood-and-fabric structures, although the principal American manufacturers wanted no part of it. German glass is now a cliché on the competition circuits of the world, but a mere ten years ago Herr Hänle felt he had to include in his *Libelle* pilot's manual a special analysis of engineering figures to reassure us that his syn-thetics wouldn't melt in American sunshine.

[2]SSA: The Soaring Society of America, Inc. Now you know why they don't call it the American Soaring Society.

Prior to the introduction of fiberglass, optimum glide ratios had long languished in the low 30s. Now, 15-meter ships were capable of delivering in the high 30s, and it wasn't long before the larger-span glass birds began approaching the magic number of 50:1. Performance on this scale, coupled with the emerging new generation of hotshot pilots, was bound to have tremendous impact on the nature of competition.

The first casualty (despite a protracted terminal illness) was that old warhorse, free-distance. The fact of its obsolescence was driven home to one and all during the 1969 Nationals at Marfa, when our Polish guest, Makula, flew 525 straight-line miles to (delightful irony!) Freedom, Oklahoma. Just about everyone exceeded 300 statute miles that day, so we lost the ensuing 48 hours of magnificent soaring weather while everyone completed tedious, expensive retrieves.

The ghost of free-distance lingers on in Paul Bikle's mutation of the task, Prescribed Area Distance or the Cat's Cradle, beloved of few besides competition directors. Here, maximum distance is still the object, but in Paul's game we fly point-to-point within a designated, limited area, with no turnpoint more than 200 miles from the contest site. While this neatly eliminates the possibility of outrageous retrieves, it almost guarantees the risk of many off-field landings, and besides, the task is still beset with most of the same inflated luck-factors that marred free-distance all along. Current guidelines call for P.A.D. only when the weather forecast is even iffier than usual. So by definition the highest premium is placed on lucky guesswork, the red-headed stepchild in modern competition philosophy.

As Marshall Claybourn put it during a briefing at Marfa in '69, "We are here, gentlemen, to select the best soaring pilot in the United States." Not the luckiest—the best.

And so, finally, the speed task around a fixed course is

coming into its own. In theory, this task affords every pilot equal opportunity to fly the same conditions of terrain and weather; the pilot exercising the skills to make the most of these common conditions earns 1000 points. When the task is properly called so that it fits the actual soaring conditions, most pilots can look forward to completing the task back at the site, with an enthusiastic reception from crews who have not budged from the field all day. Given fair and intelligent task-setting, only the inept and unlucky expose themselves to risky off-field landings, which may seem harsh, but nonetheless is just.

Of course, until we have ridden that Last Great Thermal into the Beyond, we never quite eliminate luck from our affairs. The caprice of fickle weather can make a shambles of the best-planned tasks, trapping late-launchers at the start gate, or clamping a turnpoint in midafternoon; convection may quit cold two hours earlier than forecast; and the vagaries of cirrus torment all soaring creatures, birds and pilots alike. But most modern competitors find speed tasks far less dominated by impersonal chance than any other form of aerial strife yet devised. It should also be noted that even under the flukiest conditions, a majority of the better pilots usually manage to make the best of it.

Is competition soaring, then, eventually doomed to shrivel into a mechanistic, repetitive and ultimately boring ritual of inhuman second-splitting, devoid of heart and soul? Not a chance! While there are still those who genuinely fret over the demise of free-distance tasks and what they perceive as the attendant diminution of romance in competitive soaring, I believe these mourners of the good old days refuse to face the facts and figures of modern soaring—what the past decade has wrought in terms of sailplane performance and pilot capability.

The goal we all seek, I should think, is optimum fairness with minimum regimentation. If there is any less-

regimented group of souls than a bunch of competition
pilots whistling around a speed-course, it would have to be
a cell of practicing anarchists. And when the day is done,
and you ask x-number of the pilots how things went, you
will get x-number of wildly differing impressions. Because
for any given course on any given day, there can be only
one ideal way to fly it; the poorer alternatives are literally
infinite, so no matter how short the course, no two pilots
will return from precisely the same experiences. The
closed-course race in no way restricts the important
variables, only those which might tend to allow someone
other than the best pilot to win.

True, there's no longer a place in competition for the
flower-watchers; but then, can you think of any competitive
sport nowadays in which dilettantes excel? There may be
select and rarified circles that frown upon anyone so crass as
to work hard at winning; but such an effete code, I think, is
less than likely to fire the enthusiasm of mankind. Our genes
and chromosomes simply aren't arranged that way.

Certain risk-elements are endemic to soaring, similar in
degree if not in kind to those men face in any unusual
environment—underwater, in caves, on mountains. Except
in rare cases of hopelessly incompetent contest management, the severity of risk is largely self-imposed, and can be
either heightened or reduced at the individual pilot's
option. Daredevil flying is as unfashionable in soaring these
days as it is in general aviation; through the seeding system,
major contests are closed to all but pilots of proven
superiority; and the Regionals are constantly training and
feeding new talent into the system. The thrills are all still
there for the taking—the air will never run out of surprises.
But we have learned that the greatest thrill does not come
from doing something and merely getting by with it, but
from doing it as well as it can be done. The sport is
maturing gracefully.

The greatest danger *to* the sport seems to be external—regulation and limitation imposed by outside authority with no understanding of our game, and no interest in it. Positive control ceilings are dropping faster than Chicken Little's sky; there are already vast areas of the country where it is forbidden to enter without a half-ton of prohibitively expensive electronic gadgetry aboard. The restrictions settle upon us like a lead net.

Within the sport itself, rule-making authority is wisely vested in democratic boards of representatives chosen by the pilots themselves, and very little nonsense gets past them. The machinery, like all democratic machinery, tends to move with ponderous deliberation—but it moves. Self-regulation has become such a rare privilege, I only hope we can maintain it in a country more and more begigged with little plastic credit cards, Social Security numbers and fallible computers.

We still bask in one federally-ordained distinction: sailplanes enjoy the right-of-way over all other aircraft save free balloons. It's not a privilege I ever plan to press, although I once saw (or heard) it in action.

The final task at the Chester Regionals one recent spring was a 120-mile out-and-return race with the Hickory, North Carolina, airport as the turnpoint. The day proved even scruffier than forecast, with occasional 100-fpm wisps retiring from their labors at 3000 MSL. Most of us clawed our way toward Hickory, jumping from one huge gaggle to another. Sam Francis thoughtfully alerted the Flight Service people at Hickory airport of our impending arrival.

A bit later, we heard FSS advising an approaching power pilot of our presence in the area: "Keep an eye peeled for sailplanes," said Hickory Radio. "There are four or five reported in the area."

Sam grabbed for his mike. "Hickory Radio, the figure on sailplanes is not four or five; it's FORTY-FIVE!"

"Roger on the correction," said Hickory Radio in an awed voice. Then, to the power pilot, "Cessna Four-Niner-Golf, did you copy that?"

There was a rather protracted pause, then:

"Roger, Hickory Radio. I ... er ... I think I'll land somewhere else."

There was another pause while all of us chuckled to ourselves, then an anonymous glider voice said: "Okay, fellows, I guess we'd better watch out for balloons."

Now that's *my* kind of regulation.

4

FUN AND GAMESMANSHIP

Between contests, I can think of no group more generous with advice, help and sympathy than the soaring gentry. Whatever your problem, you need only mention it and immediately you become the center of a concerned circle of volunteers who will not rest until the thing is licked. Such gallantry is even to be observed during the practice period that precedes every contest, when tools, spare parts and even crew members are cheerfully loaned back and forth between pilots busily discovering new horrors in their instrumentation or airframes. Murphy's Law ("If anything can possibly go wrong, it will") is rigidly enforced on every flight line.

Indeed, in the very heat of a contest, arch competitors will work through the night to insure that a dinged sailplane is back on the line in the morning; there is no glory in outscoring a pilot who cannot compete. Not since knighthood was in full flower has there been so much genuine concern for the woes of others.

But if you and your ship appear to be in fighting trim, you automatically qualify as fair game for the psych-artists. Since the only effective defense is a strong offense, most of us soon learn to smite before being smitten. The art of psyching didn't originate with soaring, of course, but competition pilots have raised it to new levels.

George Moffat is an unabashed psycher. Considering his track record and the overall quality of his flying, his mere presence at a contest is sufficient to demoralize three-fourths of the entrants. The hard cases he enthusiastically

attacks with a variety of weapons, not the least among
these being verbal. When an impossibly long task is called
on an obviously marginal day, most of us emerge from the
pilots' meeting moaning and groaning. Not George. If you
observe to him that the Competition Director's mother
very likely lived under the front porch and barked at
strangers, he'll nonchalantly shrug and reply, "Oh, I don't
know, I kind of *like* long tasks." Later in the day, as you
scrape and sweat around the endless course, those casual-
sounding words will constantly replay in your mind's ear,
relentlessly haunting you.

By careful prearrangement with Klaus Holighaus, designer
of his *Nimbus II*, and some crafty pre-contest homework of
his own, George and his crew ostentatiously installed
special wing-fuselage fairings and new, oversized ballast
tanks in the ship just a day or so before the 1974 World
Championships got underway at Waikerie. The effect on
the other Open Class pilots was exactly as planned:
devastating. Some tried unsuccessfully to cobble up last-
minute imitations of George's prebuilt fairings, while others
ran in a frothing rage to lodge official protests about
over-ballasting. The result of all the Moffat-orchestrated
brouhaha was an official weighing of all the ships just
before the contest opened—but none, of course, was
weighed later, out on the launch grid.

Naturally, all this psyching would be pointless unless the
psych-artist can back it up with superb performance;
George can and does.

Mild-mannered Dick Johnson has been known to visit a
competitor's spot on the grid and engage in disarming
conversation for a few moments while he runs a practiced
fingertip back and forth along the competitor's wing
surfaces. Then he'll break off the conversation, lean down
and squint along the wing, and utter a quiet "Tsk-tsk-tsk"
as he sadly ambles off. Few pilots have the strength of

character to forego a minute inspection of their wings once Johnson is safely out of sight, trying to discover the fatal flaw.

Another veteran of nerve-warfare, whose name I do not propose to enshrine in these pages, once asked me the day before a contest, "Hey, Gren, did you have any trouble with the aileron modification on Tango Tango?" I spluttered something about "*What* aileron modification?" My tormentor smoothly replied, "Oh, didn't Thomson send you the tech order from Glasflügel? I suppose it's somewhere in the mails." Under my frantic questioning, he would only reply that it was a bit too complicated to explain without the factory drawings, but that I'd probably be reasonably safe as long as I didn't exceed a 30° bank during the contest. By then, I was fairly certain I was being had; but just the same, for the next five days, every time I rolled into a thermal I was nagged by that joker's little ploy.

Newcomers to competition tend to be self-psyching. The names they've been reading about in *Soaring* magazine all this time suddenly metamorphose into living, breathing, larger-than-life individuals with sailplanes so finely competition-tuned that the neophyte is almost ashamed to assemble his own secondhand machine right out in broad daylight. Having only recently completed his Silver-C cross-country of 30-odd miles in order to qualify for entry in the Regional, the tenderfoot now faces awesome daily tasks of 200 and 300 miles, flying in the company of eagles. Around his tiedown spot, the predominating mood is one of stark, tangible terror. It takes only a couple of practice forays out into the task area to confirm his suspicion that the lift is unworkable and the terrain is unlandable, so he lies awake far into the night trying to devise some scheme that will enable him to cancel out with honor and grace, before he wrecks his beloved ship and breaks his own personal neck.

Loitering on the ramp within earshot of the biggies, he will feel his confidence, such as it is, shrinking to the vanishing point as he listens to bloodcurdling tales of what happened to old Walter at Reno, or to young Herbie at Marfa—Gothic events that transpired *years* before the New Boy took his first glider ride. Two or three days of this sort of torture will convince even the denser fledglings that they have somehow blundered into the wrong place at the wrong time. If only they knew how many butterflies were doing clog-dances in the innards of most of the old hands, too, they might feel—well, not better, necessarily, but at least a bit less unique in their misery.

A. J. Smith makes a point of avoiding practice flights with any ships that might conceivably outperform his own, preferring to shatter his competitors' composure by outclimbing and out-penetrating everyone in sight a day or so before they begin scoring. Thereafter, while flying real tasks, those pilots will expect A. J. to trounce them, and of course he does. Such little germs of doubt, properly implanted, will cause the average pilot's tottering poise to collapse, removing him neatly from any possible contention.

Moffat and some of the others derive sadistic relish from making a difficult flight sound childishly easy. After winning a task that drove most of us to the outer limits of our skill and determination just to stay airborne, George loves to report that he thoroughly enjoyed the day, never got low, and feels in retrospect that he was overly cautious on the second leg, averaging only 68 mph—this being the selfsame, miserable leg where half the field was shot down. Since he has the official winning speed to back up his story, such an account leaves most of us gasping like beached mullet.

I can see a correlation between all this and the tactics of the cagey poker player, who likes to frighten all the ribbon-clerks out of the pot early in the hand, lest someone make an outrageously lucky draw. If you can persuade most of the opposition early-on that there's no possible way for them to win, your own chances of victory are enormously enhanced; for once an opponent is defeated in his own mind, he might just as well cash in and go home to mama.

Flying skill is invaluable, of course, but it will never prevail over a pessimistic attitude. The impregnable optimism of the consistent winners is their most priceless asset, and a great many of them protect the serenity of their own souls by subtly or flagrantly attacking that of others. To be sure, all of us—even the mightiest—have assembled during our contest careers a grisly catalogue of disasters and humiliations, for such is the essential nature of the sport. We also know that so long as we persist in the game, potential pratfalls lurk just beyond every thermal. It is our reaction to this knowledge, how we cope with it, that largely determines our chances of winning a given contest.

Fundamentally, it's a question of character; if one is strong in this department, he can minimize not only the risks themselves, but the debilitating *fear* of risks, thus clearing the mental decks for full concentration on the challenges at hand. The gullible, the suggestible, the overly-imaginative and the inexperienced can be counted on to fall by the wayside with almost actuarial precision. The psych-artists don't really do them in; they only supply a slight nudge to start the avalanche of self-doubts roaring down the slopes of the soul.

Contests are the ultimate test of self-discipline. When it wavers, so does our performance; when it stands firm, the task almost seems to fly itself. Being human, most of us, we find this vital quality to be not a fixed, permanent affair like bonds in a trust fund; but rather, a volatile, constantly fluctuating business, like local stocks sold over-the-counter.

And as the self-discipline market fluctuates, so does our competition performance. They are inextricably wedded.

Perhaps the healthiest approach to immunity from psyching is summed up by, "The hell with you, Mac; I'll fly my own contest."

Easy to say, when Moffat's not about.

5

SQUAREDANCE, AND OTHER HEROINES

It's all very well to speak of soaring as a loner's game, but this holds true only for the flying part of the day. For all those gritty pre- and post-flight ground operations, soaring becomes a team sport; we lone eagles are totally dependent on our crews . . . or at their mercy, depending on the relationship.

And even while we're out flogging around the course, our crews can wield extraordinary influence over our peace of mind, or lack of it. When a pilot is blessed with a crew chief who knows what to do and when to do it without having to be told, he should daily fall to his knees and thank his Maker. For while a good crew doesn't insure victory, a poor one absolutely guarantees defeat.

I've noticed that bachelors in the competition game often turn up at contest sites accompanied by yummy-looking girls, packaged and perfumed in a manner designed to wreck homes and incite riots. Now I like to ogle and leer as much as any dirty old married man, but I've also noticed that these gorgeous sexpots tend to be largely ornamental; the actual crewing chores are usually handled by hired muscle.

We married pilots shamelessly exploit our families. We con our wives into believing that the title of Crew Chief is the highest honor to which any modern, liberated woman could aspire; every kid big enough to lift a wet sponge is signed on as an Assistant. It takes a certain flair for chicanery to establish such a ludicrous arrangement, but some husbands have sustained it for years.

There are exceptions, to be sure. I've known girls who took one horrified look at their husband's soaring site and his soaring friends, lingering perhaps long enough to observe a 98-pound wife staggering under a 130-pound wingtip—then locked themselves safely inside the car and drove resolutely home, without a backward glance. They are never seen again within miles of any soaring activity. During the week, such couples may be as one; but on Saturday and Sunday they freely pursue their separate destinies—perhaps the most civilized path around an insoluble problem.

The rest somehow find themselves hooked into serving as Chief of Ground Operations and the die is cast. Year after year, they try to wear a cheerful expression each long weekend of the soaring season while working like hod-carriers to get their men safely into the air, and safely back down again. And how they must resent those provocatively-costumed honeys who consort with the bachelors! The working garb of a real Crew Chief is as alien to the pages of *Vogue* as that of a Leningrad street-sweeper. There is simply no way for a lady wearing a stylishly brief skirt to tape the underside of a wing, and remain a lady.

There are not many ironclad axioms in soaring, but here is one: the wife who crews is a heroine. Secretly unenthusiastic, in some cases; perhaps even reluctant, but nonetheless a heroine. I have mentioned the bond that unites competition pilots; it is but a loose granny-knot compared with the ties that cement the crew-chief sorority. There is no affinity like that which springs from shared adversity, and our ladies all have the same major problem—soaring husbands. Hence, they are fated to be on intimate terms with all the deglamorizing aspects of *la vie sportive* on the contest circuit: gritty scalps, windblown hair, insects that buzz and chew and bite, sunburn in the wrong places, and the dubious delights of sharing bed and board with a walking nervous breakdown in a general miasma of dust and heat a thousand miles southwest of nowhere. A contest is neither the place nor the time for shoring up a tottery marriage.

There is only one way a pilot can possibly repay his crew for all their drudgery, and that's by winning. Since contests are fiendishly designed to produce but one winner per class, by definition all the other crews are condemned to long hours of semi-voluntary servitude in a variety of lost causes. Their slender solace rests on the hope that everyone in the family will still be on speaking terms when the damned contest is over. If our nation ever revolts against the work-ethic, the germs of the mutiny might well be traced to the ground crews of habitual also-rans.

Pilots capable of winning rarely get shot down, so during tasks their crews ostentatiously loll around the contest site, signing autographs and being interviewed by *Sports Illustrated* while himself routinely smokes around the course and finishes with a flourish for the network cameras. Pilots of smaller bore suffer nervous sweats unless their crews stay directly beneath them as they flounder across the countryside. After a few giddy hours on the highways and byways, with the rearview mirror dominated by the blank front end of a 30-foot sailplane trailer, the novelty may fade for even the most dedicated of crews. And if—or more likely, *when* their boy comes unstuck and dumps it on some inaccessible knoll, their working day has really just begun. The sheer physical demands of a retrieve can be taxing enough, God knows; but the supreme challenge at the tag end of an exhausting day is seeing that no one aboard violates Retrieve Etiquette.

The rules are pleasantly relaxed on routine, or non-contest retrieves. Most likely the pilot has simply been flying against himself—the most considerate and understanding opponent in the whole world. At the moment of landing out, he may be fuming in impotent, black rage over

the mixture of evil luck and idiot moves that have brought
him to such low estate. Yet by the time his crew arrives on
the scene, he will have rationalized the day's events quite
beyond recognition; the soaring pilot's memory is a marvel
of convenience. After a skillful bit of subconscious editing,
the most haphazard of flights becomes a glorious chapter in
man's epic struggle against overwhelming odds—the soothing
alchemy that turns dunces into heroes.

Homing from retrieves like this, a wife may fearlessly
discuss her secret dream of hiring a fulltime housekeeper or
spending next winter in Hawaii; in his self-induced state of
euphoria, her babbling mate will carelessly agree to
anything. He is so immersed in creating a respectable
fiction out of his feckless adventure he is only dimly aware
of anyone else's existence. (Later, to be sure, he may howl
outraged denials that such a conversation ever occurred.)

Contest retrieves are a rather different can of worms.
Here the opposition is neither considerate nor understanding; it is out for blood. Competition is almost literally an
acid test: I have seen it corrode men who fancied themselves fashioned of stainless steel. Much of the etching
process seems to occur during those long drives back from
off-field landing sites.

Luckily for all downed soaring pilots, there are certain
mandatory drills to be observed immediately after shunting
into the handy cabbage patch, umpteen miles from
nowhere. Unless the landing was perfect, the ship must be
inspected, heart-in-mouth, for contusions and abrasions. If
this test is passed, and the equipment seems reasonably safe
from violence by weather, livestock, rustic vandals and the
like, the pilot stumps off in the general direction of whatever signs of civilization he may have spotted on the way
down, chart and landing card in hand.

Should his luck momentarily return, he will locate a
functioning telephone nearby, confess his status to contest

headquarters, and after a reasonable wait, will see the familiar car and trailer trundling into view. The mechanics of derigging, with its frequent accompaniment of mashed fingers, sincere profanity and cathartic tears, offers welcome if temporary relief from the aches and pains of the soul; he can kick a recalcitrant trailer-fitting or vent his spleen on a stuck wingpin, and feel a lot better. While these routine chores are occupying him, he has little chance to reflect on the evil implications of his landing. (This excludes the possibility that some thoughtless competitor may have soared overhead at several thousand feet, floating serenely homeward toward completion of the task, while our man watches with clenched teeth and dying heart from his wretched field below.)

Only when the car-trailer combine eases out onto paved highway can the pilot turn his full attention to a review of the debacle. If in all honesty it was a scratchy day and he has no specific reason to believe he did more poorly than anyone else, he may briefly lapse into a state of mind bordering on the cheerful—until he thinks to switch on the car's two-way radio. (His wife has long since seen the wisdom of switching the thing off before he gets within earshot.)

Let the radio emit only random static and squelch noises for a few consecutive minutes, and the pilot will begin to smile inwardly; his grip on the steering wheel will visibly relax; he may even offer a few nuggets of information about his flight: the hopeless weather, the hotshots he remembers leaving behind at the first turnpoint, and other self-serving statistics. The crew, taut as violin strings up to now, may have a natural tendency to unwind and start behaving normally. This may not be entirely wise.

For at the first hint of a human voice breaking through the squelch on 123.3 mHz, our man will freeze, then demand: "Who the hell was *that*?"

At this moment, casual chatter is best halted. Someone should keep an eye on the road ahead; the pilot at the wheel will be leaning so close to the loudspeaker he can't possibly see where he's driving, as he strains to identify the maverick who is inexplicably still flying while *he* is reduced to mere driving. That garbled voice has made it traumatically clear that we have not, after all, made the best of a poor day; some lucky S.O.B. out there is still piling up points.

Worse still, as time passes the radio may begin yawping with a variety of voices, distorted and unintelligible, yet with a vague word here and there indicating that our day has ended very prematurely.

Then, topping a hill, a loud voice suddenly erupts from the speaker, chirping out the competition numbers of the contest goat aboard a Pratt-Read, advising the finish line that he is one mile out.

"Oh, God!" comes the whimper. "Not *that* clown!" Euphoria sinks without a trace.

If there are kids on the crew list, mother will now semaphore frantic signals to the back seat, commanding total silence and forbidding any coltish horseplay. Up front, a time-bomb ticks ominously; the least disturbance could set off a frightful bang.

The remainder of the retrieve stretches over eons and eternities. The imaginative wife may think of numerous bright remarks to ease the tension; after covert glances at the pilot's knotted jaw muscles or the white knuckles on the steering wheel, she quickly rejects them. *His* contribution to the festivities will be a feral snarl at anything, animate or otherwise, foolish enough to cross his path. In the back of the car, catalepsy prevails; white-eyed and tight-lipped, the youngsters dare not glance right or left. One, perilously close to hysteria, fights a ghastly urge to giggle, but is deterred by lurid imaginings of the doom that would swiftly ensue.

Only the Terrible-Tempered Mr. Bangs at the wheel seems unaware of the long hours since the last rest stop, but even a wet seat seems preferable to violating the high-voltage silence. Finally, gas running low, the rig is abruptly swung off the highway and into a service station; gasps of relief from all hands.

Once the physical problems have been eased, there may be a whispered conference between mother and brood near the soft-drink machine; but one glance toward the glowering pilot and the motion is tabled.

At this point, the intelligent pilot will emerge from his black funk sufficiently to realize that if he is ever again to enjoy the services of this crew, he had better relent.

"Okay, honey, get the kids a Coke and we'll split a beer," is about all it takes to end the nightmare and start the group functioning as a family again. But it is essential that the evil spell be broken by the fallen ace, and no one else.

I suppose it was inevitable, when we received SSA's blessing on "Tango Tango" as our competition identification, that the radio code for our ground station would be "Squaredance." We were amused during one of the Regionals at Chester when gossip reached us that some of the Florida crowd thought our code-word was not "Squaredance," but "Sweetass"—and they were wondering how we got away with it. So much for the quality of voice transmission on those damnably expensive aircraft radios . . . or did my dozen years of newscasting teach me nothing about diction?

In the early years, Trudy, poor dear, spent endless hours hauling the trailer along highways, or parked at hilltop service stations, while I tussled with gravity on badge and contest flights. I can't imagine why it took me so long to appreciate what an appalling waste of wife and gasoline this entailed. Since then, except in the most unusual circumstances, Trudy has stayed at the airport during my excursions, minding the radio and handy to Retrieve HQ, just in case. I realize this dandy system might not be the answer out West, where competition tasks routinely exceed 300 miles and an outlanding could involve a really tedious delay unless the crew is nearby. Here in the East, our triangles rarely take us more than 60 or 70 miles from the contest site; I much prefer waiting an hour or so in a quiet field to worrying throughout each task about Trudy and the trailer in today's irresponsible traffic.

With the onset of the fuel shortages of the mid-'70s, SSA's board of directors instructed contest officials, when setting tasks, to aim at 100-percent completions, thereby eliminating any need for ground crews to roar out and thrash up and down the highways. All were urged to remain at the site until their pilot was officially reported down, a policy of such obvious sound sense I wonder it wasn't adopted years ago. Now that we all know where our crews are, it takes just a few seconds of airtime to complete the picture:

"Hello, Squaredance." (Very carefully enunciated these days.)

"Squaredance."

"Point Two and comin' home."

"Good show."

I think there's probably much psychological merit in leaving the crew behind, whenever possible; it beefs up your motivation to finish the task when you know that's the only way to land amongst loved ones. When you're flailing about at 400 feet in zero sink and you can plainly see your crew parked beside a lovely flat field, there's an almost unbearable temptation to mutter "The hell with it!", pull the spoilers and end the agony. But if all that you hold near and dear is loyally waiting for you 50 miles away, you will fight the good fight until your wingtip brushes the broomstraw, if it comes to that.

If someone took the trouble to collect all the crewing adventures at a single major contest, it would make a great book. One of my favorite episodes involved the formidable Andrew James Smith, whose hard-bark treatment of his ground crews is legend in competition circles. Rounding up a crew for contests is a chronic problem for all bachelors, and A. J. has done little to ease his own situation; normally, his pilot-to-crew posture fits somewhere between C. O. at a military academy and Head Overseer on an antebellum plantation.

When A. J. decided to fly in a Regional at Canton, Ohio, a while back, he asked someone on the scene to organize a crew for his huge AS-W 12. The man chosen for the task was Big Walt Talalas.

Big Walt is what you could call a robust man. He sports a lovely walrus moustache, has worked all his life in the Akron tire plants, and devotes his leisure time to twin passions, beer and bowling. Neither pursuit has diminished his vigor in the slightest; he looks about half of what must be his true age.

Big Walt is not a man to be teased or casually annoyed; he seems capable of destroying a Sherman tank barehanded, and cheerfully admits his temper has no fuse to speak of. If you are his friend, you can do no wrong; if you are his enemy, you are in grave peril. We first met him when he came south to crew for his son, Walt, Jr., at one of the Chester Regionals, and found his absolute straight-forwardness both refreshing and irresistible; there is not a molecule of sham or pretense in the man.

When word spread around the Canton airport that someone with a genius for mischief had engineered this incredible combination, we figured it was only a question of time until the mushroom cloud formed.

Things started moving right along the first morning. As A. J. drove up to his trailer, he was shaken by the sight of

Big Walt with an entire AS-W wing casually tucked under his arm. "Hiya, Andy," boomed Big Walt, "Where should I put this?" (I never heard anyone call A. J. "Andy" before; neither has anyone else.)

The weather that day was patently unflyable, but an optimistic cat's-cradle was nonetheless ordained; as it turned out, A. J. was the only pilot who exceeded the mandatory 60 miles—losing radio contact with Big Walt in the process.

Due to a misunderstanding back at contest headquarters, the retrieve department closed up shop and went home just before Big Walt tried to call in for A. J.'s location. Not the least daunted, Big Walt headed for a nearby airport, where he ordered the chief pilot to take him up in a comfy Twin Comanche to conduct an aerial search for the 12. Simply by tracking the courseline A. J. was following when last heard from, they eventually spotted him and his ship, safely in a field below. After a couple of low passes to wave and indicate that help was coming, Walt and his chartered plane returned to the airport.

"You weren't planning to charge for rescue work like this, were you, friend?" demanded Big Walt of the startled pilot, as they taxied in. Something about the glint in Walt's eye helped the pilot make a quick decision: no, no, of course not, no charge at all, sir.

Moments later, Big Walt wheeled the car and trailer off the airport and sped to A. J.'s haven in the boonies, where the retrieve was finally completed long after dark.

A. J. completed all the remaining tasks (winning the meet in the process), so there were no more occasions for heroic retrieve procedures. Even so, we all kept expecting the inevitable fireworks, but it never came; A. J. and Big Walt got along like Damon and Pythias. So far as I know, they hold one another in the highest esteem to this day.

Way to go, Big Walt.

Way to go, Andy.

6

BLOW, WINDS, AND CRACK YOUR CHEEKS!

In any objective ranking of spectator sports, competition soaring would probably fit somewhere between chess-by-mail and watching the grass grow. In soaring, as in love, participation is all.

So even in a nation as bonkers over sports as the United States, soaring enjoys a comfortably low profile. Frankly, there are some of us in the sport who would just as soon keep it that way; where soaring is concerned, I readily confess to a shameless bias toward exclusivity. Naturally I'm in favor of *some* growth—so long as it's deliberate and selective: just enough new faces and wallets entering the game to keep the market expanding, so the cost of equipment stays within bounds. Numerically, we could also use a bit more clout against the chairborne bureaucracy which is bent on taking control of all the airspace . . . airspace that once belonged to birds and airmen.

Crowds depress me; those old newsreel shots of Coney Island on the Fourth of July always made me shudder. So when I hear busybodies promoting slick schemes to double the membership of the Soaring Society of America, I secretly wish them gobs of bad cess. I have this nightmarish vision of someday finding myself stuck in the middle of a long line of cars hauling sailplanes to my favorite gliderport . . . of pushing and shoving for assembly space, like sparrows quarreling over a roost . . . of waiting through the best part of the day for my turn to tow. In this hellish future, I can foresee all the biggest pastures and plowed fields in soaring country sprouting signs, visible from the air, stating in unequivocal block letters: NO GLIDERS. So please, stay away, most of you!

When we insist on obscurity, however, we invite misunderstanding. Like the stainless steel, shockproof, self-winding misconception that in soaring flight, it all depends on the wind. This non-fact enjoys more widespread and unblinking credence than the Bible and Koran combined.

As a rule, the only occasion for the general public to get a peek at soaring people and their planes occurs in those emotion-charged minutes after an off-field landing. (If the landing was adequate, the pilot is quivering with relief, while simultaneously enraged with himself and the elements for having come to such a dumb dénouement; he is also probably wondering where the hell he is.) Whether one lands in some rustic's kohlrabi patch, or on the manicured lawn of an aristocrat's chateau, the odds are a zillion to one in favor of the following question being asked: "Wind quit on you?"

Pilots who like to keep their lives simple and uninvolved force themselves to smile and agree, "Yeah, that's right." After all, how can one man hope to re-educate the entire countryside?

Yet who has never watched a buzzard slowly wheeling skyward, regardless of wind or calm? Is the mental leap from buzzard to sailplane so great? Or from buzzard flight to sailplane flight? Granted, it took millions of years for us to figure it out, but we finally saw the light: substitute sailplane wings for buzzard wings, human senses for buzzard senses, basic instruments for buzzard instincts, and behold! We fly! Well, okay, the buzzards are still better soaring pilots than we; but then, they do it for a living.

No one seeing a buzzard on the ground seems compelled to remark that the wind must have quit. One rightly concludes that the critter has found something for his dinner, or is simply calling it a day. When a soaring pilot lands unintentionally, he is simply disclosing that he is not as clever as the common buzzard; although in fairness, it should be added that buzzards occasionally cheat their way out of a sticky situation by flapping.

In the area of off-field landing experience, I don't believe I have much serious competition in this hemisphere, whether we speak of variety or just sheer numbers. I have thumped, bounced, and groundlooped into cow pastures, cornfields, unused highways, gullies, hilltops, weed patches, remote airstrips, parking lots, plowed fields—most of them places that looked much better from the air than they really were. These little forays into the unknown have cost me two broken fuselages (and one broken back) thus far; on sober reflection, I marvel that the price was so low.

If the statistics sound grim, the actual experience usually is not. Once you've swallowed the disappointment of an incomplete flight, you are too busy with practical chores (securing the sailplane, chasing off cows, horses or small children, locating a telephone, locating yourself) to brood for a while. Once all this is attended to, and the crew is supposedly dashing to retrieve you, there is usually a rather long, anticlimactic hiatus during which you have absolutely nothing to do.

Some pilots prefer to sulk in silence through these empty hours, picking maggots from their souls and otherwise tidying up in the wake of a disastrous day. I personally prefer company, which is rarely wanting at the scene of a forced landing; almost any sort of company is welcome, barring wayward, hostile drunks, or irate landowners with impoundment gleaming in their greedy eyes. If it looks like quite a long wait, I'll even tackle the wind question when, inevitably, it is raised. If there are still cu's in the sky (mocking me), I will explain that they mark where a thermal is, or was; and if they're still with me, I'll describe how we use thermal energy instead of a throttle. I know—

and *they* know—that it's all a grand waste of time, but since my time is dross until the crew arrives, at least it keeps my thoughts away from impending realities, such as tomorrow's scoresheet. The concept of vertical air currents is as alien to the earthbound as Hallowe'en on Mars. Often while I am gamely spreading The Truth, my mind's ear is previewing the conversation at a local dinner table that night:

"Fool kept goin' on about the wind blowin' *up* and *down* [coarse laughter]! Hellfahr, time I stopped the truck and seen that plane settin' there without no motor, I knew what was wrong. Wind wasn't blowin' at-all; calm as milk, it was. And him carryin' on about the wind blowin' up and down! Hee-hee-hee!" Sigh.

True enough, a moderate breeze blowing reliably from the correct quarter will result in a banner soaring day along the ridges. But elsewhere, the wind is mainly a damnable nuisance to sailplanes, the nuisance being proportional to its velocity—unless, as almost never happens, the wind chances to be blowing toward your destination.

Far from the ridges, out over flatter lands, where most of us soar most of the time, the wind bows only to gravity when it comes to vandalizing our flight plans. While thermaling, it drifts us away from course—or in the unwelcome case of a headwind, it drifts us inexorably back toward the place we are trying to leave. Strong headwind and weak lift is a truly horrid combination: at 3000 AGL, you depart a scruffy thermal over Point A, with a silent prayer setting sail for Point B; after five or six miles of relentless sink, you are so low you grab anything you can find—and what you find is another vapid thermal. Grimly, you circle in this vagrant wisp while your whiskers grow and your hair thins until you again top out at 3000 AGL—and glancing down, you are appalled to discover that you are directly over Point A again. After two or three cycles on this tedious treadmill, it is fair to begin questioning your choice of hobby.

While the wind is pushing and shoving you where you don't want to go, it also amuses itself by tearing thermals to shreds. You can be climbing at four or five knots, sassy as a jaybird, when suddenly the lift simply disappears, and you're left circling in patches of useless chop and sharp sink. A quick shift downwind may reestablish contact, but like all the other good things in soaring, it's not guaranteed. I have found thermals unaccountably shifting *upwind* at three or four thousand AGL. In the effervescent air of springtime, when both wind and lift tend to be vigorous, effective thermaling usually requires some alteration of the circle each time around; one gets a mental picture of the thermal as a sloppily-built chimney tottering into the sky, with no two courses of brick laid true and square.

Wind shear—which occurs when the winds aloft abruptly and invisibly change direction at a given altitude—also plays hell with thermal organization; at shear level, you would take an oath that you have reached the top of the thermal. Oaths of another kind will come forth when you look up and see competing pilots (above the shearline) climbing out of sight, while you seesaw maddeningly up and down in the narrow band between the shearline and Mother Earth. Any day when the cu's appear firm, flat-bottomed and trustworthy—yet you can't make it to cloudbase—you are probably the innocent victim of windshear.

Before I had given much thought to these subtleties, I had slogged partway around many a task course in a tiresome series of final glides from middle altitudes, each punctuated by a last-minute save, until eventually there would be no save and I would find myself on the ground —exhausted, baffled and disgusted. Then, waiting for my crew, I would sometimes glimpse a white wing flashing high in the sky—a sailplane smugly thermaling several thousand

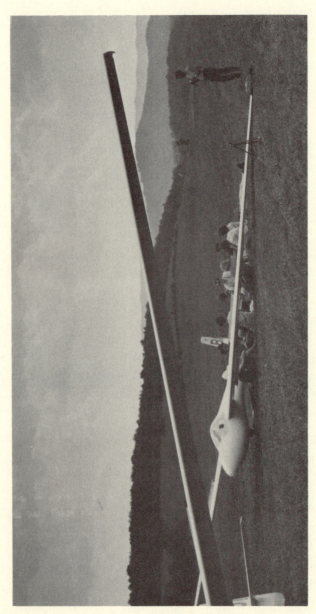

HANGAR-FLYING *AL FRESCO* AT NEW CASTLE

Soaring pilots will question why aircraft are on the ground while cu's festoon the sky above. Answer: the wind this day was gusting to 35 knots, with matching turbulence below the ridges. A good, long bull-session was the logical response.

feet above my top altitude for the whole day; my ego would dwindle to mouse-size.

So one spring recently, I decided to apply some of my habitually wasted soaring time to basic research on the windshear enigma. It seemed obvious that when cloud shadows move in a different direction from the surface wind, you have the ingredients of a windshear. On such days, I would concentrate on reaching cloudbase, even if it meant being late for dinner.

And given such a day, sure enough, somewhere in the climb, the lift would get choppy and disorganized—far below cloudbase. Under my old set of Rules for Efficient Soaring, I would have abandoned the thing with a sneer and cantered off in search of Something Better. Now, shrewdly noting the drift of cloud shadows, I nosed through the sink in that direction, and was rewarded with a couple of chirps from the variometer audio. After a bit more meaningless chop, there was an honest, renewed surge of lift, and I was on my way to cloudbase.

Of course, it's not always quite that simple, as I quickly learned. Some days I could find the errant upper thermals, some days I simply could not. If the shearline was only a thousand feet or so below cloudbase, it wasn't worth the candle anyway. But when the shearline is at 4000 and cloudbase is at 9000, the trick is somehow to bludgeon your way up through the shearline, and then try to stay above it at all costs. Above the shearline, the living is usually easy; below, it is full of tears and hardship. For reasons I don't yet understand, the interthermal sink at higher altitudes is usually far milder than it is lower down.

This sort of information, quite new to me, was probably old hat to Dick Johnson years ago, when he pronounced his famous prescription for successful cross-country soaring: *Get high and stay high*. Even the hippie cult would go along with that.

Since wind velocity normally increases with altitude, there are further judgments to be made: adverse winds aloft must be equated with rate of climb. Climbing at three knots while drifting away from course at 30 knots is ordinarily a losing proposition.

Away from the hills, then, wind is rarely the pilot's handmaiden, especially when a triangular course is being flown, which is the usual task these days whether in a contest or chasing badges. Straight-out distance flights are another matter, for here the pilot can wait for conditions that suit him. Virtually all the modern straight-distance world records (Greene and Scott, Grosse) and most of the earlier ones took advantage of tailwinds. When you have 35 knots on your tail, whether thermaling or at redline, it's a rare gift from Mother Nature of 35 nautical miles for each hour of flight. But that may be the practical limit, since winds of higher velocity would scramble the thermals beyond recognition.

Daydream: When I am in complete charge of things, my first move will be to require every billboard to carry the message, "Kites use wind—sailplanes use thermals!" Radio and television stations would be under executive orders to repeat this wisdom on every station-break; it would also become a permanent fixture on every magazine cover and newspaper masthead in the country; insolent and tardy students would have to write it 1000 times on the black-board. (I would not meddle with "In God We Trust" on our coinage, because that's a basic tenet of soaring, too.)

And you know what? No matter how long or how often we told 'em, somewhere, sometime, a soaring pilot would land out, and before he could struggle out of his cockpit, some fathead would appear, grinning his imbecile grin, and ask: "What happened, Mister? Wind quit on ya?"

7

SAILPLANE, *SI*; GRAND CANYON, ¡ *NO*!

Any pilot who has suffered lifelong from a sweaty-palm case of acrophobia invites comparison with that old thigh-slapper, the giraffe with a sore neck. *Acrophobia*, in case you've forgotten, is described by the Ph.Ds as "the abnormal fear of being in high places."

Well, in my own quaking case, it's not so much the high places that undo me; it's the abnormal fear of falling *off* of them. Ten feet AGL on our household ladder is enough to start salt water squirting from my palms, and a rather high-pitched vibration about the knees. I was once misled onto the observation platform of the Empire State Building: the longest and most abjectly miserable 15 minutes in my whole life. Scenic clifftops, picturesque ski-lifts, high-rise buildings, even those devilish glass-walled elevators in the *chichi* new hotels make me an instant coward; at all costs, I avoid them.

Such menaces, of course, are all more or less firmly attached to Mother Earth—and that's the key, at least to my own private neurosis. Get me aboard anything that leaves the earth and flies, from conventional airplane to sailplane to hot-air balloon, and I am serenely comfortable, thank you, at almost any altitude—the higher, the better. Why do I trust, say, a glider more than I trust an elevator? Frankly, I haven't the slightest notion; I simply do.

Only once in more than 2000 hours of flying have I ever felt the slightest twinge of acrophobia. In the early days of World War II, while still in college, I began learning to fly in one of those government-sponsored civilian training

programs. Parachutes were *de rigueur*; students never flew
without them. Some months later, freshly licensed and bold
as only the 40-hour pilot can be, I went up to improve my
illicit looping technique in an underpowered Aeronca
tandem Something-or-Other. At the end of a couple of
ell-shaped gyrations that I construed to be loops, I
discovered the stick was jammed full back in my lap;
despite panic pressure, I couldn't budge it. There followed
a series of near-vertical stalls, with the little plane deter-
mined to spin out of each; I was pretty busy with the
rudders while struggling with the blasted stick. When I
realized I was getting nowhere but lower, in a sloppy series
of swoops and stalls, I decided "The hell with this," and
unlatched the door and window panels preparatory to
bailing out. I already had the seat belt undone, and a leg
over the side, when some blind instinct made me reach a
hand behind my back to check that my chute was properly
attached. There was nothing there; I had taken off without
a parachute, the prerogative of student-graduates.

By now, the Aeronca had reared up on its tail-end once
again, and was starting to fall off on the right wing. For
a frozen instant, I gazed straight down at the hard winter
landscape a couple of thousand feet below my foot as it
dangled in the slipstream, and felt the icy poison of
acrophobia spreading through my system. Never before
had the ground looked so hostile or menacing to me from
the security of a cockpit; nor has it ever since.

Hastily hauling my leg back inside, I kicked full left
rudder to get the wings leveled again. As the nose fell
through a steep stall, I contrived somehow to get my right
leg behind the stick; using this leverage in addition to all
the frightened strength of both arms, I felt the stick
reluctantly grind forward to a more or less neutral position,
where it again stuck as if welded.

But by prayerful use of the elevator-trim control and a

few delicate touches of throttle, I managed a very flat approach and a bouncy but safe landing on the rolling pasture we used for an airfield. We found that a vagrant cotter pin had lodged itself in the tubing around the rod that connected front and rear sticks, effectively jamming the whole works. It took two strong men a half-hour to dislodge the offending bit.

By then, I had recovered from the external shakes; my former instructor wisely insisted that I take off immediately for a leisurely ride to restore my confidence. After propping the mini-engine, he stuck his head in the window and growled, "Remember, Ace, this ship ain't rated for aerobatics—and neither are you!"

For years, I was pretty sheepish (and therefore secretive) about this fear of falling; but in dozens of subsequent hangar-flying sessions, I have learned that many pilots share the same incongruous weakness. One of my co-victims confessed that when he glanced out of his second-story bedroom window each morning to check the weather, he had to hold onto the window-frame to avoid severe vertigo—a senior airline captain, no less. Yet we find remarkable unanimity on one point: the fear of falling attacks us rarely, if ever, while flying. It is operative only when we are at height, yet still attached to earth.

No amount of rationalizing is going to cure it, any more than a snake-hater is going to be mollified by the information that the serpent in his sleeping-bag is just a harmless garter-snake. Each of us carries some atavistic genes which defy rational analysis; trigger them, and every cell in our bodies hits the panic button. The conscious mind is quite by-passed; this is a gut reaction from pre-history.

Often, banking steeply in a good thermal, I stare down at the ground far below, and perhaps with a touch of masochism try to recapture that frozen moment of terror

30-odd years ago when I almost made my terminal fall. But
it's simply not there, not at all. There have even been
moments when my aircraft was temporarily but totally out
of control—literally falling down the lee side of a ridge, or
slamming through the indescribable violence of a rotor-
cloud—situations terrifying of themselves, yet never tainted
with that old nemesis, acrophobia. I trust the fluid air
eventually to resume its laminar flow across and beneath
my wings; order will be restored.

I wonder, now, how many acrophobics have shied from
flying because of the logical suspicion that airplanes are as
frightening as cliffs and high buildings. Many, I suppose;
and more's the pity that most of them won't have the
luck, or the nerve, to find out differently.

8

THE VIEW FROM DOWN UNDER

Winter is the nemesis of North American soaring pilots. Granted, it gives us a chance to refamiliarize ourselves with hearth, home and polite society; read the mail, pay the bills and pet the dog. But the blah season of short, blustery days and long, frozen nights often seems to outlast spring, summer and fall combined.

Some years ago, in a brilliant stroke of genius, Ed Byars and Bill Holbrook hit upon the idea of creating their midwinter *Soaring Symposia*, to give the frozen fraternity one long weekend's respite from chilblains of the soul. Their faculty glistens with the great names of soaring— national and international champions, technical pundits, sailplane designers, everyone in the sport worth listening to.

Lest all this expertise prove too massive a dose of perfection, I was called upon one year to address the *Symposium* banquet, with instructions to present the lay (or loser's) viewpoint.

I'm going to talk a little tonight about soaring from down under. If you think that has anything to do with gliding in Australia or New Zealand, forget it. I'm talking about the typical contest scoresheet, and my typical place on it. After losing more than a dozen contests in a row, I'm beginning to suspect it isn't entirely the result of flukey conditions. So all this winter I've been reviewing the doleful record to see if any sort of pattern emerges. So far, I've only been able to conclude that my flying has been . . . well, consistent.

Like most pilots, I believe that if I treat my sailplane right, it will treat me right. So my ultimate goal is to let it stay in the bedroom with me between flights; but, of course, not until I can provide a nice, comfortable hangar for Trudy.

To an outsider, a remark like that might create the impression that some of us regard soaring as something above and beyond a mere hobby. But that's simply a matter of semantics; what do you mean by "hobby"? If you think that Michaelangelo's hobby was fooling around with marble, or that Attila the Hun enjoyed vandalism as a pastime, then you could properly say that soaring is our hobby.

I will confess that I've always found it easy to distract myself from the earnest demands of making a living. But not until I began soaring did I realize that I could squeeze honest work into such a tiny corner of my life. Perhaps if I moved my desk and typewriter into a windowless basement room, I could get in a legitimate six or eight hours at a stretch. But when I glance outside and see those fat little cu's growing into fat *big* cu's before high noon, all the humdrum responsibilities of life sort of fade into the background. I rationalize that I can build a lot more character up there than I can down here.

I'm sure you've observed that all the really good soaring weather comes in the middle of the week. This probably explains why so many of the soaring pilots we know are either self-employed professionals, or top-level business executives. They're the only people who can disappear from their desks on Tuesdays and Wednesdays without having to explain their absence to some lump of a boss who thinks that if you want to go flying you buy yourself a ticket.

An interesting figure recently from SSA: only 346 of us flew in the various contests in this country during the past two seasons. This leaves a bit more than 97-percent of

SSA's active membership apparently standing on the outside of competition looking in.

But I think it's a big mistake to measure general interest only in terms of active participation, especially in a risk-sport where you have to lay it all on the line. After all, there's just a handful of active astronauts in the country, but when they're doing their thing, the whole nation holds its breath and watches, enthralled. That's a sort of stretched-out analogy, granted; when Neil Armstrong goes soaring, the networks and wire services couldn't care less. But the point I want to make is that competition is the leading edge of the whole soaring movement. Aside from attempts to set new soaring records, I don't know of any other circumstances that promote ten-tenths flying like a contest. And while, obviously, only a few hundred of us care a fig about participating in 10/10ths flying ourselves, there are thousands of non-competitive soaring pilots who fly with us vicariously, sharing in our occasional triumphs and our magnificent failures, albeit from a safe distance.

And were it not for pressure on designers and manufacturers to create sailplanes that can outperform other sailplanes, we'd all likely still be floating around in *Minimoas* and *Weihes*. So it seems fair to suggest that our noisy critics, the contest-haters who enjoy peaceful weekends in their unscarred glass ships with L/Ds of 40 or better, might think it over before they knock the very phase of the sport that made such ships possible.

A while back, somebody came out with the charge that competition was breaking up soaring families. Hogwash! Name any other sport where you could find a grown man in the middle of a big plowed field, sobbing on his wife's shoulder; and his wife sympathetically saying, "There, there, dear—Doctor Steinhoff and Steve duPont landed even before you did." I hope I don't sound chauvinistic when I say I can't imagine a wife worthy of the name who would abandon her man, knowing that he may be on the brink of suicide at the end of any given task.

It is also alleged that competition brings out the worst in us. Nonsense! Only after I'd flown in a half-dozen contests did I *begin* to learn how to pray with conviction and sincerity. Now, during any contest, I'm practically a one-man religious revival. I'd be just as happy if they skipped the pilot's meeting, and held a prayer meeting instead.

I guess there'll always be a good deal of misunderstanding about this sport of ours. I've got a friend back home who fooled around with us at Chester for about half a season one year, then sold his ship and quit cold. When I asked him why, he gave me the usual list of problems—too many other outside interests, no time left to be with his family, and all that guff. And then he said: "Actually, Gren, it's nothing but an ego trip." This from a man who'd never been more than one thermal away from the airport!

As you and I know the hard way, there's nothing like flying in a soaring contest to restore a man's humility. I always find the drive back home from a contest takes a long, long time, no matter what the actual distance may be, because I tend to spend the whole trip performing a detailed autopsy on my latest performance. The time does not glide swiftly by when you're plucking the maggots out of your soul.

Dear Hearts, I have been abusing my backside in sailplane cockpits for close onto 1300 hours now, and speaking as I do from an endless series of misadventures, I can state with authority that the sailplane is the most haphazard form of transportation anyone has devised since the high-wire in the circus. I will bet you even money that if I quit shaving for a week and dressed up like a convict, I could *hitchhike* around the average "speed" triangle faster than I usually make it in my speedy soaring machine.

I was born and raised with an average American-sized

ego: I pretty much went where I wanted to go and did what I wanted to do and life was nice and relaxed. Now there's a sailplane in my life and I can hardly remember that old straightforward way things used to be. When I started soaring, I was a laughing, carefree fellow in the prime of life, confident that this would be a provocative little challenge to keep me amused during warm weather. Since then, I've spent most of my spare time pitting my brains against gravity—which in my case is like going up against a battleship with a cap pistol.

I try to picture myself as David, of David *vs*. Goliath fame. But of course, David *won*—and that's the part I can't seem to get the hang of. So my poor ego has been steadily dwarfed, miniaturized, and shrunk until today, it would look puny next to an electron.

But at long last, after all those ill-fated cross-country ambitions, and all those embarrassing contests, I'm beginning to grasp some basic facts I should have seen years ago. For instance, have you noticed how each year we have this brief, elite list of winners, and a great, sprawling mob of also-rans? And how little traffic there is between those lists, season after season?

It is appropriate that we chiefly hear the voices of the masters at these conclaves. These are the magic lodestones we losers would hope to touch, and by some alchemy of the soul be transformed into snarling tigers, eager and ready to go forth and win! Thus, each February we come panting back through slush and sleet, to sit at the feet of the superstars and soak up some more of their secrets.

But I've noticed something about that, too. Each year, I learn a bunch from these people. But then the teachers go home, and I go home, and when we all meet again at a contest, they have somehow managed to learn a helluva lot more. So my relative position on the smart-ass list stays right where it always was.

I believe our faculty stars really lay it on the line
when they tell us how it's done. But I've lately come to
realize that after you've hung on every word uttered here,
and then gone home and committed the entire proceedings
to memory, and then thought about it all very hard, you
know what it all boils down to? They're telling us they win
by not losing; so we're right back at Square One. Not that
they don't try, bless their superior hearts. Old George and
A. J. and the rest have been showering us with pearls for
years. But I wonder if asking a champion how he does it
isn't sort of like asking a beauty queen how she got so
pretty. Well, sure, she had to learn to walk that way, and
smile that way, and fix her hair and all . . . But what really
drives the boys straight up the tapestry was originally
installed by God, and He hasn't given any interviews lately.

If there's one thing that's absolutely essential to keep a
fellow interested in soaring, it's optimism. This, of course,
does not apply to the habitual winner. In fact, a good way
to tell who's going to win a contest before it even starts is
to listen around and find out who's doing the most crying
and moaning and bitching. Your real winner plays the
congenital pessimist. Talk to the man before the contest
and you'll get the saddest litany of woes since Job retired:
nothing on his panel works properly . . . his ballast tanks
leak like puppydogs . . . the start gate is at least 500 feet
off . . . the Competition Director is criminally insane . . .
his crew chief has Parkinson's disease . . . You know the
pitiful songs you hear from these dudes. Then they go out
and clobber the bejesus out of everyone.

And while the winners are breaking our hearts with all
their wailing and carrying on, how do the soon-to-be losers
sound? Like a goofy bunch of crickets on a warm hearth,
that's how they sound. Your day-in, day-out loser is not
only immune to the lessons he might learn from his own
discouraging history; he also has this insatiable appetite for

humiliation. But above all, he is bolstered by an uncrushable optimism. As each contest approaches, he hypnotizes himself into believing that this time it won't be so bad—and of course, it's even worse.

Would you believe that after my first couple of contests, I was innocent enough to think I had committed all the idiocies possible? And that from then on, it would probably be just one big triumph after another? Of course, I have since discovered that I possess an unlimited talent for creative contest-blowing; never the same way twice, is my rule.

Back in those early days, I had a direct, no-nonsense method. I would find some way to get myself shot down on the first leg of the first task, a good long hike from the nearest rabbit-path, so there would be no hope of a retrieve before midnight, and thus no way to relight. This way, I placed myself about 900 points behind the leaders in a single master stroke. After that, I could allow myself to make some reasonably intelligent flights, for no matter what I subsequently scored, I was firmly planted among the 1-26s[1] and DNCs[2].

But no true artist is long satisfied repeating the same old pattern. I find it's much more spectacular to create a catastrophe after several days of passable flying. In fact, there are times now when I get this weird feeling that I'm just a helpless, innocent spectator as I go hurtling along to inevitable, ultimate humiliation. I think some huge, invisible, evil force takes control of my contest flying. Somewhere out in the contest area, "it" plants a few

[1] 1-26: A delightful little single-seat transitional trainer manufactured, since the memory of man runneth, by the Schweizers in Elmira, New York; also comes in kit form. These little birds boast about the same glide ratio as the average buzzard. Never mind, the 1-26-ers fly their own National Championships each year, and reportedly it's a blast.

[2] DNC: Did Not Compete, a sad entry at the bottom of scoresheets, usually connoting a broken sailplane.

horrendous boo-boo's with my name and contest letters on them—like aerial booby traps. And while I may seem busy with my smart little stratagems and clever little tactics, when I suddenly stumble across one of these poisoned opportunities, I embrace it with a glad cry, and promptly find myself going down in flames.

Now it should not be assumed that I fly this way all the time. On practice days I often approach perfection. I have made sparrows envious with my saves. I have seen practice turnpoints from so high up they barely showed on the film. I never get lost; my radio works like NBC; tow pilots compliment me on my smooth flying; and groundlings who don't know any better time me around the course, as if it mattered.

Then they get out the official stopwatches and plug in the computers. I can always tell the instant this happens; no matter where I am, I get this stomach cramp. From the moment we begin playing for keeps, I am a new, but not a better man. Don't bother me, please, after a contest is underway. I am busy composing a great symphony of disasters, and it makes me temperamental as all get-out.

It figures that any sport based on the notion of staying airborne by finding some hot air has got to have its moments of vexation. For me, the low moment each morning of a contest occurs when yesterday's hero is up there in front of the pilots' meeting, telling us with studied nonchalance how he zapped around the course at 89 mph, while the rest of us were enriching the tow pilots with four or five relights apiece.

He will reveal that after a few routine phone calls to meteorologist friends in Bangkok, Thailand, and Nome, Alaska, it was perfectly clear that in order to make any sort of speed at all, you'd have to clear the start gate sometime between 1302 and 1304. And of course he didn't head straight for the first turnpoint like the rest of the mullet; oh no, he flew 'way off course to a big, blue hole; and just as he expected, he found a good street of blue thermals, so he didn't circle at all for the first seventy miles. And so on and on, until I'm ready to totter outside and throw up.

During these nauseating recitals, I often wonder if the winner and I were really flying the same task on the same day. One thing: we did not see the countryside from the same vantage point. My own view of contest terrain is usually from quite close-up. When you do a lot of your soaring below 1000 feet, you find you get a real feel for the texture of the land ... how the crops and livestock are getting along ... and best of all, people wave at you. Below 1000 AGL, who needs an altimeter? When you can tell whether the girl waving down there has a nice complexion, you know damn well it's time to stow the map, drop the gear, and start hollering on the radio for your crew.

I've always been a great booster of pre-flight planning— and one of these days I hope to get a chance to do some of it. Unfortunately, I seem to be one of those people who are constantly victimized by inanimate objects. The H-301 *Libelle* is famed far and wide as a docile, obedient, thrifty and loyal little ship that goes out of its way to make a pilot look good. And as long as I'm just trying to outclimb a gaggle of student pilots in 2-22s[3] and such, good old Tango Tango adds luster to the *Libelle* reputation.

But under the duress of real competition the poor little ship just goes all to pieces. Thirty minutes before launch time, the main tire will decide to go flat—have you ever

[3] 2-22: Another of those timeless Schweizer creations, a dual trainer in which legions of American soaring buffs took their first instruction and flew their first solo; ungainly and unlovely, lumbering, with a performance like a homesick brick, they are nonetheless almost indestructible, as befits a trainer, and brimming with charity for all but the most grossly inept student. The 2-22 belongs right up there with the Jenny and the Stearman in the annals of flight training.

tried to fit an American bicycle pump to a metric tire
valve? It just lies there and hisses at you. Even the trailer
gets jumpy; in the midst of assembly, I've known it to lash
out and inflict a nasty scalp wound. Or during ballasting,
one of my wingtanks decides to burp, and I will fly that
day with three inches of water sloshing about the cockpit.

In college English, I learned that when a writer ascribes
human emotions to inanimate objects, it's called "pathetic
fallacy." Well, what happens is pathetic all right, but what
I'm telling you is the truth. So with this Chinese fire-drill
going on each day in my assembly area, I always figure I'm
lucky just to get airborne, ready or not. Mostly not.

May I mention one more little thing the winners do that
annoys me? When they talk about their brilliant in-flight
decisions, they always manage to sound like third-genera-
tion computers straight off the IBM shelf. To each situation
they bring inspired insight, cool deduction, and a calculat-
ing mind that spits out logical solutions like a Gatling gun.

In my own cockpit, the picture is somewhat different.
The scene is basically one of supreme chaos. In the first
place, I always have trouble flipping a coin in such
restricted quarters; and if I drop it under the seat, I never
find out what the answer was. At other times, I become a
sort of one-man debating club, producing instant and
persuasive arguments for and against every possible move.
While this fascinating intramural discussion takes place, the
altimeter is doing what comes naturally—unwinding.
Rationality eventually yields to hysteria, and I may wind
up threatening some innocent plowed field a few hundred
feet below: "Okay, you damn field, either give me a
thermal or I'm gonna land on you!" If the field knows
anything about my landing technique, it will usually kick
up a hell of a good thermal.

I have no firsthand knowledge, but I suspect that over
the long haul winners find soaring pretty dull. By defini-

tion, only the losers experience the true melodrama, the pucker-up-and-pray situations. If you persist in staying high and flying fast, you get a sort of astronaut's view of the contest; all you really need is a WAC[4] chart and something amusing to do each afternoon after you've smoked across the finish line.

Only those of us who achieve compound catastrophes—who are afflicted with an infallible instinct for disaster—come home with memories that will color our nightmares for years to come. We're the guys who always manage to reach the cu's as they begin their death rattle . . . who arrive at the bottom of the big gaggle just as the lift quits completely . . . who have struggled like insects in amber against that great unseen hand that forces us down into the boondocks . . . We're the ones who instinctively follow highways because they play such a big role at the end of our day's flying . . . and who but us ever gets to shake hands with all those stimulating farmers and scintillating deputy sheriffs?

So now there's a brand new competition season looming ahead. If there was a corpuscle of realistic blood in my veins, I would block up my trailer, throw away my glider button, and start writing jokes for the *Embalmer's Quarterly*. Spring would come and flow imperceptibly into summer; summer would pass predictably into fall with no foolish trips to unlikely places; no sleepless nights in plastic motels; no overcooked steaks and warm salads and cold eggs. I could give all my credit cards a well-earned rest; tow pilots would no longer rub their hands greedily when they

---

[4]WAC: World Aeronautical Chart, a relatively small-scale map with few terrain or cultural details, chiefly used by affluent power pilots accustomed to gobs of horsepower, speed and altitude. Sectional Charts, covering about eight statute miles to the inch, are the preferred navigational crutch for soaring. Helpfully visible items such as open-pit mines, major highways, railroads, etc., are displayed with lavish abandon. Yet even Sectionals are not foolproof, as witness the day I wandered 20 miles off course on a 45-mile leg; there seems to be something about thermal flight that raises my natural proclivity for disorientation to fever pitch.

spot my name on an entry list; there would be one less minnow for the big fish to overtake and devour. Right now it almost sounds tempting.

But when the season gets underway at Chester in April, I think we all know perfectly well who's going to be tugging his little white bird out to the launch grid, overflowing with foolish high hopes, telling himself, "This time, it's going to be different! Boy, this time the old home team's gonna show 'em how it's really done! No more messing around in weak thermals, no more wishy-washy flying, no more friendly visits with Mother Earth. Today it's all going to be high and fast and a new course record, and fame and honor, and at least a footnote in the history of soaring." And after listening to this interior jazz concert for a while, I'll even have myself believing it.

And if out on the first leg that afternoon you should happen to look way, way down and see a tiny white *Libelle* grinding around amongst the tall pines, with no hope of lift and no place to land, ask not for whom the bell tolls, Friend; it tolls for me.

9

A SHORT CONTEST

After seven lean years of humiliation and an almost perfect string of defeats in sundry contests, this was the moment that had colored some of my most wistful dreams: standing before a pilots' meeting at a National Soaring Championships, telling all these aces how I had contrived to beat the lot of them the previous day. The reality was every bit as delicious as I had envisioned; I dragged it out as long as I dared.

After I finally sat down, Competition Director Sam Francis decreed that henceforth, pilots describing their winning flights could not exceed the time required for the flight itself. [Unseemly, raucous laughter.] But that's not what really deflated my ego—it was the knowledge that I had merely won a practice task. On the official score-sheets, I was still zero, like everyone else.

The date was Tuesday, June 19, 1973—opening day of the Standard Class Nationals at Chester, South Carolina. Following my spellbinding account of the previous day's outing to Laurens, S. C., and return, Sam said it was going to rain and therefore he was declaring a no-contest day. And did it rain? Yes sir, yes sir, three bags full.

It had been raining all month; some days, it just rained harder. One of the pilots who showed up three weeks early for practice growled: "Maybe we ought to check on the Gulf of Mexico; it's probably bone dry."

Another gasped: "If I have to spend another afternoon in our motel room, I'll be too weak to fly."

The next two days were also washed out. As a

consequence, I still had the best flight of the non-contest and I made the most of it, edging up to any group of pilots I spotted and hanging around with an air of phony modesty until someone relented and asked me to talk about it. Soon people were running at the sight of me; there was no one left to talk to but Trudy, and she went sound asleep.

Sic transit gloria mundi.

After three days of rigging and then derigging, or not even bothering to rig at all, the launch line was actually open for business on the fourth day of the meet. Meteorologist Ed Paquet had consulted his charts, soundings, sequence reports and the sky itself, and had brought forth a forecast of marginally soarable weather. Sam and his committee posted a modest, 88-mile speed task to Lincoln Airport and return.

What almost never shows up on charts, soundings, sequence reports or the sky itself—until it is actually happening—is a local line squall. A lucky half-dozen pilots who chanced to be at the head of the launch sequence and didn't dawdle around the Chester area before starting, made it to the turnpoint and back out again before the squalls struck.

The rest of the field found itself being shot down at various points along the course between Chester and the town of Lincolnton. The squall line was absorbing most of the energy in the area. As several pilots approached its leading edge, they found strong lift—glassy smooth in some areas, violently turbulent in others—up to 700 fpm. Once beneath the line of storms, though, it was all relentless sink. A few who came immediately behind the early starters managed to squeak through the sink and land straight-in at the turnpoint, with inches to spare. Those of us who came a bit later found the turnpoint blocked by

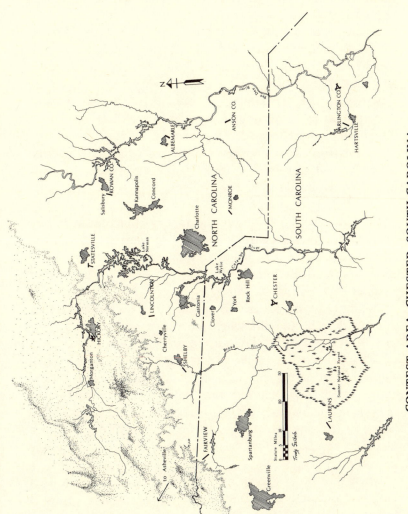

CONTEST AREA, CHESTER, SOUTH CAROLINA

heavy rain, the approaches buffeted with high winds; it was unassailable.

To make a contest day, the rules called for 14 pilots to cover at least 60 miles; with the storms slicing across the courseline, it wasn't even close. Four days down, six days left—and officially, we hadn't even flown yet.

With all the outlandings, there was only one serious mishap: in an odd double accident, my beloved Tango Tango was almost totaled.

Except for two compressed vertebrae which still give me an occasional stab in the back, it seems today almost as if it had all happened to someone else.

He flew two-thirds of the distance to Lincolnton before he found a thermal strong enough to work to cloudbase, which turned out to be something less than 4000 MSL. *Well*, he heard his mind's voice saying, *I'm glad they didn't stick us with a long one today*.

Passing east of Kings Mountain, he checked the courseline on the chart: right where he was supposed to be. But just north, toward the turnpoint, the whole sky was darkening into an ugly black curtain as a line squall mushroomed along an east-west axis and slowly drifted south. He switched on the radio, and from all the miscellaneous chatter his ear selected the voices of two pilots instructing their crews to leave Lincolnton and head back south. *Somebody*, he thought, *got there before the storm*.

Then he flew under the leading edge of the sinister clouds and found lift: 200 fpm at first, but as he circled it increased ... 300 fpm, 500 fpm, and up to 700 fpm just before the scud began to blot out the inky ground below. While climbing, his radio had been crackling with terse announcements from pilots on final all up and down the course. *How many had made the turn*? he wondered, over and again; and there was no way of knowing.

At 4000 he made his decision, diving away from cloud-base, heading north under the heart of the storm-cell, where he found the black underbelly of the cloud hanging hundreds of feet lower than the upswept leading edge. Here all was turbulence—he dared not exceed redline—yet he dared not lose sight of the ground. Finally, he cleared the last trailing wisps at 3000 and leveled off. As the airspeed dropped from 110 knots to 70 he watched for the down-pegged varios to swing back to a more normal reading. They didn't budge.

A few miles ahead, he had glimpsed, end-on, a slender north-south strip that might have been Lincoln Airport. But now there was heavy rain; the canopy was opaque ground glass and straight-ahead vision was hopeless. As his altimeter unwound like a berserk clock, he slewed the ship around so he could study the strip ahead more carefully through the side-vent of the canopy.

No, Lord help us, that's not Lincoln Airport or any other airport, but it will have to do. Directly below, the sparse fields were steeply pitched against the hillsides; there were powerlines everywhere and trees whose leaves showed their silvery-pale undersides in the violent wind gusts.

What had looked, through the storm and at a distance, like an unpaved airstrip, now turned out to be some sort of grainfield with a narrow swath mowed down the center, 55 or 60 feet wide and no more than 300 feet long. *Why in hell don't farmers mow the whole bloody field while they're at it?*

In rational air, it would have been an easy glide with a thousand feet to spare. But in this eerie down, he was beginning to worry about two sets of high-tension lines slowly rising on the canopy between him and the tiny field. He crossed the first set, the huge steel pylons rising beyond either wingtip, and dived for the second, lower lines. Then they, too, were behind him; ahead lay the field. By now the rain and sink had both moderated, but there was not enough altitude left for him to circle and study the problems. This would have to be that most dangerous of games—a straight-in landing in an unknown peapatch.

While his mind automatically gauged the space he had to work with, the dive-brakes nibbled at the pitiful surplus altitude so he could touchdown at the absolute edge of the field. After all that rain, this field—even though stubbled— ought to be soft. Leave the gear up, jam it on the deck, and let the belly slosh into the mud and stop itself. (Thought and decision in less than a second.)

There is still surface turbulence, he realized an instant too late; *GET THE WING UP*! even as the left wingtip dipped and grazed a few inches into the verge of the three-foot-high unmowed crop. As he felt the ship cart-wheel horizontally, his mind's voice was saying, "*Another foot ... another lousy foot!*" For a long instant the sail-plane was hurtling backwards, then came tremendous shock and awful noise as the tailskid dug into thick clay. The ship seemed to lunge backwards in a series of separate leaps, the fuselage absorbing punishment it was never designed for. Inevitably it yielded—a clean break just forward of the empennage, the horizontal stabilizer chewed to shreds, the roar of dreadful destruction amplified in the stunned cockpit. The ship ground along for 60 feet or so, strewing gear doors and gelcoat and balsa and fiberglass bits along its backward path. The muscles between his shoulder blades had spasmed; *God but this hurts.*

Then it all stopped, the left wingtip on the ground, covered with mud; his eye noted brown straw tightly packed into the flap-aileron joint. He tried to twist around to see how bad the tail was, but found he was virtually paralyzed. His wind was knocked out; each time he tried to gasp for breath, his back muscles would spasm again. The inner dialogue continued in chatty fashion: *Well, Old Timer, you have really done it this time.*

Then he saw the second sailplane, coming directly at him. *He'll never make it*, his mind's voice observed matter-of-factly; *this damn field isn't big enough for* one *ship*.

Numb, shocked and disbelieving, he watched the oncoming sailplane until it filled the whole sky, banking at the last second to swerve a few feet to his right. He felt his ship leap and fall back under him as the other plane's mainwheel impacted with his right wing, out near the tip. Simultaneously the second plane's wingtip flashed across his canopy, six inches above his head. He was too paralyzed with pain and fright even to duck. Then behind him he heard the unmistakable sounds of a fiberglass sailplane thrashing to a stop in a violent groundloop.

Looking at the impacted right wing, he saw the flap and aileron compressed and twisted beyond recognition. Midway to the wingtip, ruptured fiberglass and balsa shard protruded from the monocoque skin where the spar had been smashed.

Sure was a short contest, said the talky voice in his head.

"Sure was," he replied to himself in a choked whisper. "It sure as hell was."

During the days that followed, the pain in my back gradually grew bearable (only after a full month of Trudy's devoted nagging did I finally visit a surgeon and learn the extent of the damage). By tacit agreement with Sam Francis and his right hand, Jim Herman, I became an *ex-officio* member of the Competition Committee; since I brought a total vacuum of previous experience to the job, I suspect I learned a lot more than I contributed. Yet just hovering on the sidelines was something; I never considered going home.

I also discovered how a grounded pilot feels when the rest of the troops are out slogging their way around a tough task; it is not habit-forming. I was genuinely touched by words of sympathy and condolence from just about everyone connected with the contest, but as the bumper-stickers say, I'd Rather Be Flying.

For the next five days, we had a soaring contest. A barely perceptible improvement in local weather permitted a Cat's Cradle, a couple of speed triangles, and two goal-and-return tasks with optional turnpoints, a new wrinkle in 1973. The highest speed posted for the contest was a shade below 53 mph, which gives you some idea.

Had my admiration for the spirit that motivates competition pilots needed any reinforcement, it would surely have gotten it during that hot, hazy, cloudy and humid June week in piedmont South Carolina. From my uncomfortable perspective of groundling, I could only monitor the contest frequency for snatches of pilot-to-pilot comment, painting mental pictures of the countless difficulties that faced our 50-odd guests day after day. The general impression I still carry from that week is best summed up by the old-fashioned word, gallantry.

Take Dick Schreder's save:

"East of Gastonia, I got down pretty low, and I couldn't see anything in the sky that looked like lift, so I drifted over toward this big power plant on the edge of Lake Wylie. There were five big smokestacks and they were all putting out some smoke. By the time I got there, I wasn't very much higher than the tops of the stacks—and you know, when you look right down into those things, they are huge!

"Anyhow, I lined up on the stacks and started to fly across them and almost got knocked out of the cockpit when I crossed the first one; it kicked me up maybe 20 or 30 feet, but I completely lost control of the ship in the turbulence. By the time I had things back under control, I was over the second one, and again everything went hay-wire. But each time I saw I was picking up 20 or 30 feet

Tom Beltz' Std. *Cirrus* crossing the finish line.

Competition Director Sam Francis and Rusty Dishongh; Rusty Dishongh, Ellen
and Glenn Maxwell at start gate sight line; Sam Crane at start gate window.

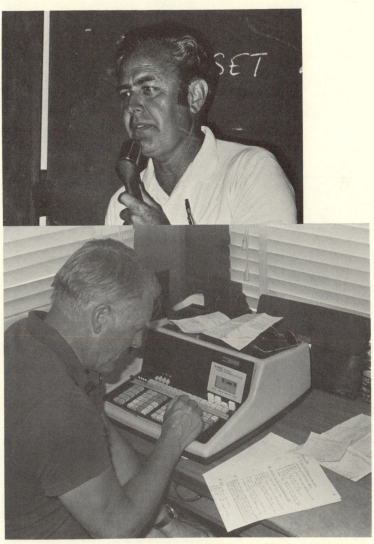

Meteorologist Ed Paquet; Chief Scorer Jim Herman.

Contest Manager Joe Giltner and A. J. Smith; pilots' meeting.

Pre-launch activity.

Fritz Sebek's daughter, Nancy; George and Suzanne Moffat; Rob Penn and Trudy Seibels; the Moffats and Ralph Boehm.

Bob Fergus' Std. *Cirrus*, flown by A. J. Smith.

Sam Francis and Dick Schreder; Jim Herman and Ed Paquet.

Paul Bikle; Suzanne Moffat; Dick Schreder.

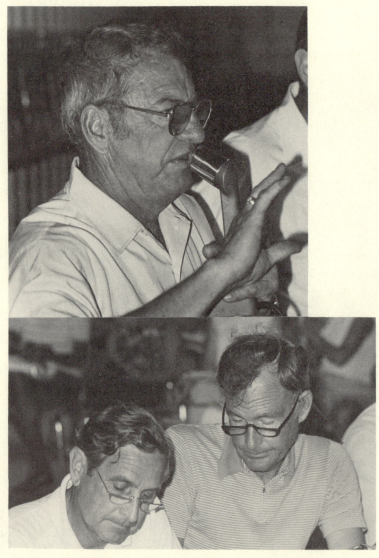

Joe Giltner; George Squillario and Ben Greene.

George Squillario and Ben Greene; Steve duPont; Karl Striedieck and Jim Smiley.

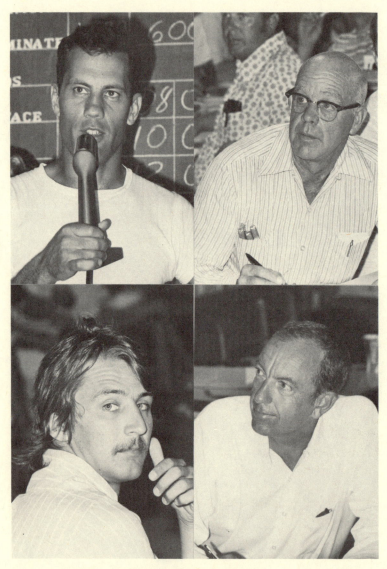

Karl Striedieck; Paul Bikle; Tom Beltz; A. J. Smith.

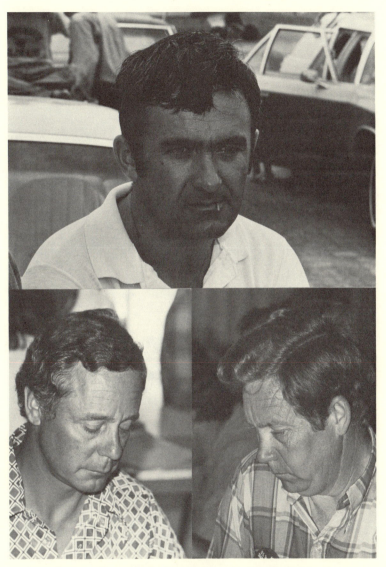

The Happiness Boys: Jim Smiley; Art Hurst; Ed Sessions.

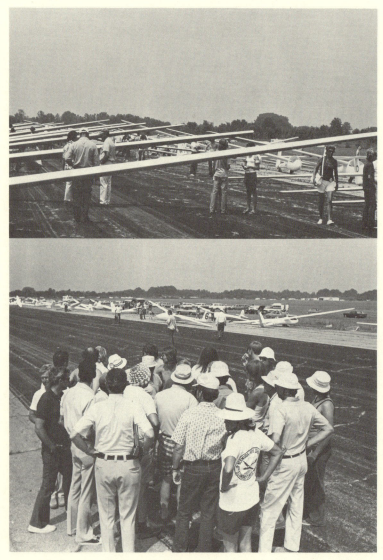

Launch grid; weather update.

Weather briefing; Ben Greene, Ice Berg, George Squillario.

Dick Schreder swinging compass; A. J. Smith and Robbie McCormack.

Herbie Mozer and crew; Ed Sessions pumping ballast.

Tom Beltz; Ed Byars; Paul and Alan Bikle, A. J. Smith.

Big John Brittingham; George Squillario.

Ben Greene; Ed Byars.

Janice Hoke, Dave Culpepper; Gayle Coffman, Sam Lyon.

Ben Greene, Std. *Cirrus*.

George Moffat, Std. *Cirrus.*

The late Quentin "Ice" Berg, Std. *Cirrus*.

Karl Striedieck, AS—W 15.

At the finish line: Paul Bikle's *Nugget*; Ev Williston's Std. *Libelle*;
Woody Woodward's Std. *Libelle*; Ed Sessions' Std. *Cirrus*.

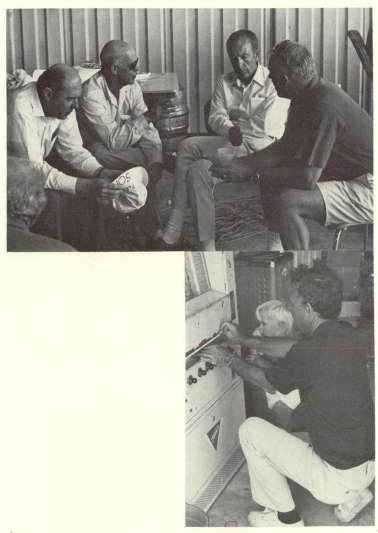

Sam Francis, Paul Bikle, A. J. Smith, Jim Herman; Ben Greene and Neil Smiley.

Liars Dice: Donn Calder, Big John Brittingham, Ed Byars, Bill Holbrook, Paul Bikle; Solvi Smiley, Bobby Bowden, Jim Smiley.

H301 *Libelle* at ease.

Contest Director's trophy; The Winners, tenth through first: Bill Holbrook, Ed Sessions, Paul Bikle, Carson Gilmer, Ben Greene, Big John Brittingham, A. J. Smith, Tom Beltz, George Moffat, and Karl Striedieck, U.S. Standard Class Soaring Champion, 1973.

Photo by Rob Penn

LS—1D thermaling near Chester.

Individualists to the core: a final view of the winners.

Photo by Rob Penn

whenever I hit the smoke, so after I'd made the first run, I turned around and made another.

"There was just no way to control the ship in that hot smoke until I had run through it enough to gain some altitude. Finally, I was able to set up a regular thermal circle and rode back up to cloudbase at 600 or 700 fpm.

"But I'll never forget how big those smokestacks seemed when I first looked down inside them from 20 or 30 feet above!"

For some reason, the first ship across the finish line always arrives alone; after that, they seem to finish in little bunches.

Today, it was Jim Smiley, smoking in over the trees from the northeast, skimming the grass as he whistled across the line at something on the far side of redline, then chandelling up with the big red Alfa Hotel showing on his tail and under his wing.

A group of us—a few legitimate workers and several drones—lolled on portable lawn furniture around the sightline at one end of the start/finish gate. It was over 90° and the water-cooler flowed like wine. Two workers, perched on top of the derelict schoolbus that marks one end of the line, binoculared the northern horizon for more finishers, but for a long time after Smiley's textbook finish none appeared.

"I have a butterfly ten feet out," called Mike Hoke.

"Bad finish—he's going the wrong way," said a pundit.

There was only the sound of crickets in the shimmering heat, and desultory conversation from the sweating bodies that languished at the end of the 3300-foot line bisecting the airport infield.

Thirty minutes later, the radio roused itself with the voices of a half-dozen pilots, in fast sequence announcing themselves one mile out. Some came high, some came low, nearly all at redline, and thus nearly all crossed us with that jet-like, dopplered, whistling rush of a sailplane being flown flat-out.

"Mark!" said Rusty Dishongh at the instant each hurtling white nosecone intersected the sightline. A second or so later, his voice would come floating back to us across the field from a loudspeaker outside contest headquarters. Then: "Good finish, Xray Xray," or whoever, and these words would also float back to us like an electronic echo.

There would be another long pause for cricket identification, and then another covey of finishers.

This was one of the optional-turnpoint tasks; Rusty was asking each finisher to disclose his turnpoint on the radio, so this and the elapsed time could be relayed via field telephone to Jim Herman at Contest Headquarters. Jim fed it into the Wang computer and had each pilot's average speed before the pilot had time to land.

When Rusty put the question to Ed Byars as he

approached the finish line, he responded in a voice laden with fatigue:

"Statesville, North Carolina .... or Chicago, Illinois; one or the other."

It had been a long day.

Another day; mid-contest—late afternoon, almost dusk. Since nearly everyone finished the task, the ships are all back in their boxes along the tiedown line, save for the unlucky few who went down somewhere out in the boonies.

Big John Brittingham has netted some fresh mullet and is reopening his Liars Dice Symposium in the main hangar, directly behind Sambo Giltner's ever-popular draft beer concession. Losers pay off in rounds of beer; Big John estimates he will have to stay on in Chester for at least a week after the contest is over to consume all the beer he's already won.

Over at the portable trailer that serves as contest HQ, Jim Herman has been poking figures into his trusty computer and has just posted unofficial daily and cumulative scores for the top twenty pilots. This bulletin attracts a swarm of contestants looking for their names and positions, along with the inevitable contest statisticians who like to play with the numbers and try to forecast the ultimate winner before the flying's all done.

In Retrieve Headquarters, one of the volunteer ladies is patiently confirming route instructions from a hapless pilot whose crew is still hours away: " ... A quarter-mile *beyond* the cotton-gin?" she asks. "All right—a dirt road a quarter-mile past the cotton-gin where the mailbox says 'Snopes'—is that right?" (Has one of our boys landed in Yoknapatawpha County?)

A bit later, we are inhaling gin-and-tonic outside the

Moffats' tent, which is deep in the woods behind the tiedown line. After the long day's heat, the pines are green and cool; but it takes at least three strong gins to restore the fluid balance.

We are comparing Chester with other contest sites. George and Suzanne are impressed with the friendliness of the townspeople; it reminds all of us of Bryan in '71.

"Small-town specialty," I venture. "Where the locals all know one another, the outsider is usually treated with great courtesy as soon as he is properly introduced."

Suzanne comments: "The people here remember you and speak to you the second time you visit their stores." Then, laughing, "I've been buying groceries at the same place in Elizabeth (New Jersey) for five . . . no, six years now, and I don't think a soul in the place has ever spoken to me."

Watching Suzanne gracefully deal with the lime wedges and Schweppes bottles, I ponder on the state of manhood in Elizabeth, where such a girl could go unnoticed.

Suddenly, Trudy and I become aware of mosquitoes arriving outside the Moffats' tent for supper; it's time for us to leave. Strolling back to our car, it occurs to me that on this day George has very nearly been nudged out of first place in the scoring. Previously, I had always thought of a front-runner in his non-flying hours as a cross between a snapping turtle and a scorpion, touchy as nitroglycerine. Yet here we've been lolling around with George reminiscing and chuckling as if there wasn't a contest within a hundred leagues.

Relaxation! That's the secret, I tell myself: hang loose, tranquilize, worry not.

And—who knows?—this may well be part of the winning formula. But like so many of the secrets of superior soaring to which I am privy, knowledge is one thing—execution another.

Once you become an official DNC, you find yourself

scanning the daily scoresheets with a cool detachment denied active contestants. I knew every pilot, and most were close friends. But in the aftershock of the accident, something inside had gone a long way off; in the midst of a major soaring contest, I felt remote and isolated.

Yet even while licking my psychic wounds, I observed— as from a great distance—as Karl Striedieck stormed his way to the top in five days of inspired soaring. He had built his previous reputation solely on what he calls "ridge-thrashing"; no one at Chester was prepared for the enormous versatility he displayed that spring above the gently rolling flatlands of the Carolinas. The grit developed during twelve-hour ridge flights appears to have its competitive uses as well.

In this sport there are no overnight stars. George Moffat, forced to settle for second this time, was in his eleventh year of soaring when he won his first U. S. Nationals (Marfa, 1969).

Then there was young Tom Beltz, who had seemingly come from nowhere to win the Standard Class title at Marfa in 1972. There at Chester, Tom placed third— statistically unimpressive unless you consider the roster of veterans he demolished in the process: A. J. Smith, John Brittingham, Ben Greene, Paul Bikle ... and a long, imposing list of others. Yet those of us who had been flying the East Coast competition circuit for the past few years weren't all that much surprised by Tom's "sudden" success. Time and again, flying an archaic Standard *Austria* and still in his 'teens, he had consistently humbled his elders, who were much more experienced and much better equipped. His cumulative performances at Marfa and Chester (at last aboard a new Standard *Cirrus*) won him a slot on the American team which flew in the Internationals at Waikerie the following winter. When the elders gather to shake their heads in envy, it's not just a matter of Tom's great talent; there's also his youth. When many of us have been hung up on the hangar wall in senile retirement, God forbid, he will still be in his twenties.

It was to be ten months before my *Libelle* flew again. The Beltz family had an extra car at Chester, and they graciously volunteered to trailer the bits and pieces north to New Jersey on their way home.

It has been said that no man is indispensable; whoever said so didn't know Art Zimmerman. His was the muscle, brain and heart behind the *Concept-70*, perhaps the most ill-starred sailplane venture in the history of U. S. soaring. From his native Germany, he brought years of experience in the fabrication of strong and beautiful forms from epoxy and fiberglass; he also brought a dream of breaking the European monopoly in competition sailplanes. Against immeasurable odds and almost single-handedly, he designed and produced the first all-fiberglass, high-performance sail-plane in America.

The prototype was rushed to the Nationals at Bryan (1971), semi-complete and hopelessly unready for serious competition. I remember Art laboring around the clock beside the big hangar, heroically trying to cope with the growing list of squawks from the pilot after each test flight. The ship was withdrawn from competition early in the meet.

At Minden, Nevada, the following year, a decently finished *Concept-70* was entered—but the ship's evil star glittered on. A careless crew failed to safety the wing-pins; during the subsequent high-speed run through the start gate, as most of the nation's top competition pilots watched, the wings separated from the fuselage; the pilot parachuted to safety. The ensuing inquiry completely exonerated Art's design and construction, but it took months to complete and publish . . . months during which no new orders came in, and a few of the existing customers evaporated.

Art kept the business alive by faith—and repair work. He cheerfully accepted wrecks no other shop would touch. Patiently, he would cut into the mess and probe until he found structure that was sound; then he would rebuild and shape and form and grind and sand and polish until the owner himself could not point with certainty to the damaged area. His standards were those of the Old World perfectionist; you could fly with supreme confidence anything Art rebuilt.

Perhaps it was the toll of all those years, battling alone against fate's entire repertory of dirty tricks: Art's great barrel of a body began to sicken—slowly, at first, then with a plunging momentum that dismayed his family and friends. Disdaining the pain, he journeyed to Atlanta to address the 1974 Soaring Symposium. Briefly, we discussed the final stages of Tango Tango's rehabilitation; then he began enthusing over his latest design concept: a sort of articulated wing whose leading edge could be adjusted vertically, permitting the pilot to select the best angle of incidence for any given airspeed.

"And I know how to make it, Gren. I can make it reliable and I can make it not too expensive. It will *do* everything that trailing-edge flaps are *supposed* to do, except for landings!"

Then the gleam in his eye faded, and in a voice gone flat he said, "But I am too tired; I am too old." He was not yet fifty.

A month later, arriving at Art's little factory at Lake Swananoa, New Jersey, to bring Tango Tango home again, we learned he had been hospitalized, desperately ill.

On an April morning during the Region Five contest at Chester, the message was brought to our trailer: Art was dead. The usual commotion of the pilots' briefing was abruptly silenced when I made the announcement; then, reacting to the unbelievable, I heard many pilots breathing to themselves, "Oh, no!"

Mine was the last sailplane Art repaired. If that is a distinction, it is one I would dearly wish to forfeit, from any standpoint, if only I could.

10

CU'S AND THE CRYSTAL BALL

Scarcely had we gentled the sad, broken shards of *Tango Tango* into its trailer and returned to Chester when Tim Kelly and Leo Buckley, top honchos of the Blue Ridge Soaring Society, materialized at the contest site and began circling around me like vultures eyeing a yummy carcass. Skipping diplomatic niceties, they came straight to the point: since I was going to be grounded for the rest of the season, how about running the Region 4 contest for them, come Labor Day week? Naive, trusting and innocent, I acquiesced, "Why not?"

My five-day stretch in the hot-seat at New Castle, Virginia, was one of the most instructive experiences of a lifetime. And of many lessons learned, one towers above the rest: the person who usually gets the least sympathy during a contest, yet deserves the most, is the Competition Director. To pilots who have flown in many a contest but never run one, this may smack of heresy, but I will not yield one micron; I have been there, and I know.

Prior to that eye-opening episode, I had shared the popular belief that when you thrust an otherwise amiable, reasonable sort of person onto the Competition Director's throne, Jekyll becomes Hyde—a hard-hearted, glinty-eyed troll whose chief joy in life is to set tasks nobody can complete. I had pictured him cackling with demented glee whenever pilots called in to report off-field landings.

It turned out to be one of those scary jobs in which you assume a great deal of responsibility under conditions over which you have almost no control—conditions like terrain and weather. The New Castle gliderport snuggles into one of the narrow valleys that separate the main chain of the Appalachians from the subsidiary Blue Ridge Mountains. East of the Blue Ridge system, the land gradually wrinkles into the coastal plains. But around New Castle, in all directions, the terrain is mostly diagonal, and some of it is vertical. On a clear day, with strong, high thermals, it is the most picturesque soaring site imaginable. Toward the end of every summer, sad to report, southwest Virginia is prone to languish in a stagnant, hazy, immovable air mass. During previous Labor Day contests sponsored by my friends in the Blue Ridge group, I had seen visibility well below VFR minimums without a cloud in the sky. Poking your way around in this sort of glop, you can make several turns in a thermal before realizing you've joined a gaggle. Navigation is mostly a matter of hunches, and you can usually count on a low inversion layer to clamp what little convection the haze permits. That kind of weather over that kind of terrain makes for an interesting contest.

Yet one of the most reliable axioms we learn in soaring is that the best lift is found over the highest ground. Hence, when the day shows signs of coming unglued, you'll always see the old pro's heading for the hills—if there are any hills handy. This tactic calls for a certain amount of grit, since there are rarely any landing spots on the hills themselves, or anywhere near them (in case the axiom is out to lunch).

The problem facing the task-setter at New Castle, then, lies each day in deciding whether to send the troops along and across the ridges, gambling that better lift will offset attendant terrors; or to point them southeast toward the flatlands, where the lift may be scarcer but the terrain is friendlier. For three days I stuck to my high-ground principle, and the pilots came back each afternoon a bit white around the eyes—but they came back, the most of

them. The next day, forecast to be a real boomer, I
relented and opted for the "safe" country to the southeast;
that was the day not one contestant got back home. By
sundown, I had drained the sour cup of embarrassment. As
the first retrieve crews and their pilots came splashing
across the ford and thumping up the dirt road to the
airfield, I ran to intercept them and express my regrets; but
from the stony stares, I sensed I was not getting through to
them, somehow, and retreated to my medicinal bourbon-
and-branch. It was like reaching out to a hungry puppy and
being bitten.

Let me not count the times when I have found myself
grinding around in some teasing wisp of zero sink, merely
postponing for a few minutes the inexorable visit to a
pasture—and heard a string of cusswords pass my lips,
followed by the name of the incumbent Competition
Director who got me into this fix. Never again! On every
competition task, I now realize, there are three people
intensely concerned about my safe return to the contest
site: myself, Trudy, and the guy who sent me forth.

Intuition had already suggested it, but only after facing
the grim responsibility of setting tasks during a stretch of
rotten soaring weather did I fully appreciate how utterly,
even hopelessly dependent the Competition Director is
upon his forecaster. I never openly accused my met man of
getting his dope from some back issues (*circa* 1873) of the
Farmer's Almanac, and perhaps it was just as well; after
three or four days, I concluded I was dealing with a
psychopathic liar. I didn't want to be the one to push him
over the edge, so I humored him. After going through these
motions on the telephone, I would then halve his good
news, double his bad news, and formulate my own forecast.
By the end of the contest, my system was beginning to
work nicely.

Hastily, before my many good meteorologist friends put

me on the NOAA "enemies" list, let me add a few sympathetic words of understanding. Our Big Uncle in Washington has yet to concede that accurate weather forecasting depends chiefly on plentiful observation data. Our existing network of observation stations suffers from a critical case of gaposis; in many areas, stations may be hundreds of miles apart. This may be good enough for the Big Picture delivered on our TV sets—"Partly cloudy and warm, 20 percent chance of showers today"—with the major fronts and air masses neatly drawn and labeled. But what's happening in those huge gaps is anybody's guess. It's in the gaps where we do most of our flying.

Ideally, the Competition Director strives to set tasks that will fully exploit each day's weather; that's why he is at the mercy of the forecaster. If the met man inclines to be optimistic, the C. D. will naturally tend to overcall the task, moving smartly to the top of every competitor's hate-list. Undercalling tasks, which results from overly conservative forecasting, is a lot more popular with unthinking pilots, but it can be equally deadly to the success of a contest: a short task flown on a strong day produces bunched scores, with no significant point-spread to show for the day's work.

We are currently blessed with a handful of professional forecasters—Chuck Lindsay in Washington, D. C., and Ed Pacquet in Columbia, S. C., to name two notable examples—who completely understand the soaring pilot's admittedly special needs, and can foretell with uncanny accuracy what he will encounter out on course three, six, even nine hours later on. With men like these on the contest team, everyone has fewer problems. The C. D. can put away his Ouija board, and the pilots can start letting their fingernails grow out again.

I suspect the Lord has it in mind to see that weather forecasting always remains more of an art than a science; and this could be one of His blessings in disguise. While

I—along with every other sweating, frightened soaring pilot—would applaud a huge leap forward in the accuracy-average of the average met men, I'm not so sure I'd want the whole game reduced to infallible, computerized efficiency. Carried to its logical extreme, we would know beforehand where every thermal on course would be located; its strength, its duration, its useful upper limits. And knowing this, where would the sport be?

However, the average level of our present-day forecasting gives little immediacy to such a threat. Many Regionals, and even some Nationals, blunder along with meteorological intelligence that ranges from barely adequate to grossly inept. Little wonder, then, that the first two or three tasks at some contests turn out a bit weird; it takes that long for a Competition Director to size up his forecaster and begin applying the necessary correction-factors to his prophecies.

I have noticed that the first-class forecasters devote every evening to debriefing as many pilots as possible, thus obtaining a practical picture of the day as it actually worked out. By comparing this information with their forecast data, they begin to get a feel for local peculiarities of terrain, convective patterns and other special characteristics of the area. Like good pilots, they learn something valuable from every flight, every day; and when this is fed into their next computation, the resultant forecast is apt to be even more trustworthy.

But when a weather briefing is underway and you are told that the trigger-temperature won't occur for two hours, yet you can see cu's dotting the skies outside, you have just learned something worthwhile—not only about the weather, but also about the weatherman. Be prepared to do your own meteorology for the rest of the contest.

And yet, despite the wild inaccuracies built into the system of task-selection, competition pilots are the kind of breed who often make the task-setter look good by actually completing overlong courses on days when sensible hawks and buzzards are grounded. Such ordeals are not much fun in the doing, but there is enormous post-flight satisfaction in beating the odds by finishing an impossible assignment.

If I am lucky enough to make it all the way on such a day, I confess I pay little heed to the official scorer's numbers. Privately, I award myself 1001 points and a big "E" for enduring.

11

A SAILPLANE, BY ANY NAME

"Ships," in the gospel according to George Moffat, "is the name of the game."

George was speaking to Byars' and Holbrook's second Symposium on Competitive Soaring. He had just won his first National Championship at Marfa, Texas; the following summer, he would return to harvest his first World Championship. We listened attentively.

Many of us in that audience had flown against George; we therefore knew what it's like to be trounced, to put it as charitably as possible. Yet there were some secret doubters present who didn't entirely agree with him then, and don't now—myself included.

Because I suspect that George, along with the elite few who can be considered his peers in soaring, could spot most of us five L/D points and still hammer us into the ground. Since the top pilots always fly the best equipment they can lay their hands on, we may never see this suspicion confirmed, but I'm going to cling to it just the same. It doesn't really ease the pain, it just spreads it around a bit.

All other things being equal, the best ship would always win. But all other things are never equal, which is what makes contests interesting and final scores sometimes astonishing: Ray Gimmey's win at Minden, Nevada, in 1972, aboard a Standard *Libelle*, against a vast field of 18- and 20-meter Opens. Art Hurst outflying 50 Open Class ships in his Standard *Cirrus* at Bryan in 1971. Bill Holbrook winning the 1974 Smirnoff Derby in a ten-year-old, 15-meter H301 *Libelle*. These magnificent examples of man-over-machinery leave some doubt in my mind that polar curves are the ultimate deciding factor.

Now obviously, if you insist on campaigning some toad of a ship that converts a three-knot thermal into zero sink and gobbles 600 fpm at 75 knots, you're not going to give the competition much concern. As the 20-meter pilots learned to utilize the mind-boggling performance built into their hefty birds, the good ones had little trouble winning by the numbers over so-called Open Class ships in the 15- to 17-meter wingspan range; David *vs.* Goliath upsets soon became rarities.

The truly competitive pilot doesn't care a fig for equality, except as it applies to the rest of the field; for himself, he wants every edge he can contrive this side of disqualification. It thus becomes a matter of utmost importance that rules governing the game be clear, intelligent, airtight and enforceable. For only when we square off with ships of reasonably equal performance, as we should in fair competition, does piloting become the chief factor in the contest, as indeed it should. Flying a sparrow against a peregrine falcon is neither sporting nor instructive.

For the past quarter-century, we have been flying in one of two major leagues: Open Class ships of unlimited wingspan, whose designers were free to prank around with any performance- and safety-enhancing device they chose; and Standard Class, limited to 15-meter wingspan and festooned with several other restrictions that have been a constant source of contention since they were imposed over two decades ago.

Through the 1960s, the choice between Open and Standard Class was mainly a matter of personal taste, since the cost differential wasn't very significant. Most of the top-drawer pilots opted for Open simply because the ships flew better, and the Open Champion was considered the real, National Champion. Standard Class ships flying in the

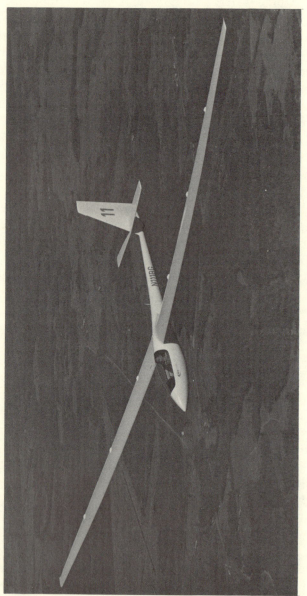

THE GREAT WHITE OVERCAST

Ben Greene cruises his mammoth, 20-meter AS-W 17 near the Chester airport (hazily visible under his right wing). Optimum glide angle approaches 50:1, but the cost of this beautiful bird and its competitors is far beyond the means of most pilots.

Nationals suffered from a Little Brother syndrome; they were stigmatized with an asterisk on the scoresheets, and while the highest-scoring Standard Class pilot won a medallion, the group had to weather a lot of snobbery.

Economics suddenly changed that picture. These days, if you're shopping for a competitive Open Class ship, and you're an American of better-than-average affluence, be prepared to peel off about two years' gross income before buying your first tow. The performance is sublime, but the cost is ridiculous ($28,000 and up at this writing); there is a growing consensus that the Open Class—or Unlimited, as it has recently been dubbed—may disappear from the U. S. competition scene within a decade, or less. We may find ourselves adopting the syndicate method for fielding two of the big birds in the biennial World Championships, with private trials and eliminations being conducted by an SSA competition committee to select ships and pilots. Only millionaires need apply.

By 1975, the (Open) U. S. Nationals had evolved into a Dual Class contest, with a handful of well-heeled (or over-extended) pilots competing with one another in the big ships, and a horde of average citizens enjoying what amounted to a contest-within-a-contest aboard 15-meter machines. Despite flukey exceptions, there could be no meaningful competition between the two groups. All of which explains the dramatic, overnight rise in popularity of the National Standard Class Championships after its inception in 1970.

Despite incessant tinkering with the rules, many pilots came to regard this contest as the only significant test of flying ability in the early 1970s. Standard Class machinery is no longer cheap, either; during the recent years of world-wide inflation, the price has nearly tripled. But the growing market for the smaller ships helped keep the tab within rational limits, whereas the demand for the 20-meter behemoths has dwindled to a precious few. Aside from economics, there are other attractions for the 15-meter set: rigging and disassembly are so easy that a pilot can usually manage with a single crew member; performance is good enough to make them fun to fly; and most of them are highly competitive, one design against another.

What everyone hoped for, all along, was that we might reach that charming plateau in sailplane evolution—in Standard Class, at least—where it no longer mattered what you flew, but only how you flew it. Trouble was, the state of the art kept racing out 'way ahead of the rules.

For those unversed in the politics of sport aviation, a brief exposition: the Federation Aeronautique Internationale (F.A.I.), with headquarters in Paris, is the Big Daddy-Rabbit of worldwide sport aviation. Gliding falls under the jurisdiction of a branch of the F.A.I. known as the C.I.V.V. (Commission Internationale de Vol à Voile). The National Aeronautic Association (N.A.A.) represents the F.A.I. in this country; and the Soaring Society of America (S.S.A.), in turn, attends to soaring matters for the N.A.A. Dull, but important.

Back in the 1950s, the C.I.V.V. established the original Standard Class concept, with the laudable intention of promoting the design and development of 15-meter sailplanes that would be safe, simple and cheap. Therefore such frills as retractable landing gear, flaps, drogue chutes, water ballast and the like were all prohibited. Safe, simple, cheap.

Human nature being what it is, each of these worthy goals was eventually trampled in the concerted rush by designers and pilots alike to attain better 15-meter performance. From time to time, under fierce prodding from manufacturers who were reacting to fierce pressure from their customers, a reluctant C.I.V.V. gradually repealed most of the original Standard Class restrictions (but not all). Retractable landing gears were approved some years ago (instantly consigning every fixed-gear ship to obsolescence); then, speed-limiting spoilers were scrapped in the face of blatant, unrepentant non-compliance by all the West German manufacturers, which came to light in 1970. Next came approval of simple trailing-edge flaps in lieu of spoiler/divebrakes; water ballasting also got the nod. And so it has gone—by fits and starts, a nearly total revision of the initial concept until finally, we had a large class of aircraft (over 300 in this country alone) that are complex, expensive and by no means as safe as they might be.

Each rule-change triggered a painful upheaval in the 15-meter ranks; to stay competitive, you had to change ships almost annually. Plainly, the ultimate goal toward which the C.I.V.V. was fitfully lurching was a 15-meter sailplane with no restrictions other than wingspan; but they were trapped between advancing technology on the one hand, and owners of the existing worldwide Standard Class fleet on the other. This Gordian knot was finally resolved in mid-1975, when Bob Buck, representing the United States at a Paris C.I.V.V. session, neatly floor-managed adoption of a new package of competition classes that recognizes the realities of modern soaring without trampling any existing equipment into oblivion.

When the dust finally settles, we will be flying in three—perhaps four—classes instead of two, covering everything but manned kites. Open will continue as is, of course, but it will be called Unlimited. Existing Standard Class ships that meet the 1972 definition (no flaps being the chief criterion) will fly against their peers in a Standard Class that should be stabilized until the planes wear out. There may even be a "Club Class," eventually, which will hark back to the original Standard Class definitions of 25 years ago—fixed gear, low but safe performance, no frills.

And most importantly of all, the C.I.V.V. legitimized a 15-Meter Class—other than wingspan, no holds barred. The delightful design concept that was born in Eugen Hänle's kitchen more than a decade ago can finally emerge from behind the bar sinister and take its legitimate spot in the sky. All these years, the H301 *Libelles*—more than 100 of them—have been the red-headed step-children in competitive circles: too sophisticated to fit into Standard Class, too small to compete realistically in Open. Now they can take on the new generation of 15-meter ships with interlocked flaps and ailerons and for the first time fight on even terms. We can anticipate a flock of new birds from West Germany and other producing nations—exciting little 15-meter gems sporting all the design and technical brilliancies hitherto repressed under the Standard Class code. It takes no crystal ball to guess where the action is going to be during the next decade of soaring.

It was a very long time coming, but the C.I.V.V.'s bold action apparently resolves, at a stroke, all the significant weaknesses and conflicts inherent in the two-class concept. No existing ship has been rendered obsolete; competition can at long last be conducted between aircraft of like performance; and designers can address themselves to any of the four sanctioned classes, secure in the knowledge that no capricious rules change can threaten their work before production begins.

If one of the longest-running hassles in soaring has finally been put to rest, we need fear no dearth of others to fill the gap. If you enjoy acrimonious debate, just mention landing flaps to a German soaring type—or a Britisher, a Belgian, a Swede, or whoever. Most Europeans, for unfathomable reasons, harbor deep, dark suspicions about using fully-deflectable trailing-edge flaps on sailplanes—flaps that can be lowered 70° to 90° for steepening the final glideslope and slowing the touchdown speed. These happy effects are enormously attractive to anyone who has ever had to choose between a small field and a smaller one . . . anyone who flies on the western side of the Atlantic, that is. But most of our European friends remain obstinately against them, despite their routine use on virtually all powered aircraft built since the Ice Ages.

As I dimly perceive it, their argument runs something like this: Suppose you are landing, eh? And so already your landing flap, she is down, *non?* And just at the last moment, you see that you are—how do you say it?—under-shooting, *oui?* What can one do? If one *ups* the flaps, *certainement*, one is sinking straight into the ground! If one *doesn't* up the flaps, one is sinking straight into the ground! *Mon Dieu*, but this is madness! (All of this to the accompaniment of that uniquely Continental gesture of despair—shoulders shrugged, eyes rolling, palms turned out.)

And, as with most misconceptions, there's a germ of truth in what the man says; this sort of thing could conceivably happen, but only to a "pilot" who has no understanding of the proper use of flaps when there's no throttle handy. With minimal instruction and practice, one soon learns never to grind in full flaps until he absolutely *knows* he has the field boundary made with some altitude to spare. He would probably milk the flaps a bit in the pattern, sloughing off obviously excessive altitude, but no one in his right mind would commit himself much beyond 20° of flap until he was looking straight down at whatever obstacles must be cleared. Then, on with the full schmear, point your nose at the near edge of the field, and drift gently down at a remarkably steep angle, flair, and touch down at a fast trot. For those who've tried it, it's a vivid improvement over a fast, shallow approach with full spoilers, then watching two-thirds of a tiny field race beneath the wheel before it can be cajoled into making contact at an exciting 40 knots or better.

The art of safely placing a large sailplane inside a small field—especially a field whose edges are trimmed with tall trees, utility poles and other devilish devices—is unquestionably the most demanding in all of soaring. We need all the help we can get. Yet the alternatives to landing flaps all have severe, even critical, limitations.

Spoilers (synonymous with dive brakes) used to be fairly effective for glide-path control when they were located across the center-of-lift, and were hefty enough to hold a sailplane at its placard redline speed in a vertical dive. But after the Germans unilaterally defied the rules and got away with it, spoilers were quickly moved to the aft portion of the wing chord, where of course they are all but useless: away from the center of lift, they have little effect on glideslope, but they do manage to increase the touchdown speed by several unwanted knots.

Drogue-chutes, like flaps, permit a steepened glide-path over obstructions without increasing airspeed—when they work. Tango Tango's drogue-chute failed the first time I tried it (it had been packed by Ben Greene, who had been using chutes for two years); luckily, the failure occurred at Chester's huge airport, so nothing was lost but face . . . and any chance of 100-percent reliability. A year or so later, the damned thing failed again—this time in a real-life off-field landing.

We were flying an informal task during a weekend of soaring in the Great Smokies of western North Carolina. After scraping along for some 20 miles without finding a thermal worth mentioning, the only flat field I could reach curled along a bend in the Nantahala River just outside a small mountain village. The approach would have to be over some very high, very potent-looking transmission lines from the local power station. As I crossed these with a respectful margin, I yanked the lanyard to deploy the drogue-chute, simultaneously nosing down for the expected steep, slow glide into the field. It was steep, all right, but when I leveled off I was doing about 85 knots—something was wrong with the chute.

Even with full divebrakes, I was obviously not going to get the show stopped before hitting a highway embankment, complete with utility poles and wires, now just a couple of hundred feet ahead. Still flying, I began tapping the wingtips on the ground to induce a groundloop of sorts. On perhaps the third tap, something caught; the ship slewed sideways, the gear dug into the fortunately soft loam, and under a shower of black bottomland soil we came to a stop with the tail pointing straight at the highway embankment, some 20 paces away.

After a few deep-breathing exercises, I struggled out of the cockpit and did the usual heart-in-mouth walkaround, but there was no damage at all. While waiting for Trudy and the trailer, I trudged back along the curving field, searching for the missing drogue-chute. Not until I was standing almost beneath those 24,000-volt transmission lines did I spot it—swaying gently back and forth in the breeze, the canopy looped around the topmost line. Instead of deploying, it had jettisoned.

Hookup error? Cockpit error? I'll never know. It was three days later before the local utility people were able to borrow a mammoth cherry-picker from the TVA and pluck the errant chute from the huge power line. They kindly mailed it to me in a dress box.

Since then, I have learned to plan my approach to tight landings as though the chute were going to fail, rather than relying on it to do most of the job; I try to avoid selecting fields that would be feasible *only* if the chute functions properly. Used in this fashion—as icing on the cake instead of the cake itself—the drogue can soothe much of the sting during pilgrimages into small fields. But without 100-percent reliability, I will never feel entirely comfortable with drogues; and they can be absolutely hellish when landing crosswind.

Back when Standard Class definitions were the top priority in soaring discussions, I was kicking the subject around one day with Paul Bikle, who asked: "What's so magic about 15 meters? If you're going to junk all the other restrictions, why not junk that one, too?"

I admit I had to think about that for a while, because there are several answers. First off, 15 meters seems to be the minimum span for adequate performance by today's competition standards; despite the huge success of the fun-filled 1-26 Nationals, not many pilots would go overboard for a 12- or 13-meter Unlimited. Yet the moment you go beyond 15 meters, you encounter a sharply rising curve of structural, weight and cost problems—the very problems that are combining to put Open Class out of nearly everyone's reach. So while 15 meters sounds like an arbitrary figure, in practice it has proven to be a very good one.

Sailboat racing provides the healthiest example for our rule-makers to emulate; for any given class, the rules are simple, straightforward and ironclad. From the smallest and cheapest to the biggest and most expensive, enforcement of the rules for each class is evenhanded and relentless, so that no matter how much a competitor is willing and able to spend on equipment, cost is not the sole measure of performance. The importance of human skill is preserved.

It seems to me that this is what soaring competition is all about—or ought to be.

12

LUCK, BE A LADY

If there's any pursuit more likely to keep a person's ego in check than soaring, I don't think I want to hear about it. Granted, in any sport we're going to have some off-days—it happens to the very best. But an off-decade? I seem to be working in that direction.

I think it only meet and right that newly-hatched fledglings should suffer more downs than ups. Yet, prowling around the Chester area in my supposedly high performance ship, occasionally I encounter some raw student thermaling in a rented 1-34. *Fish in a barrel*, whispers my undernourished ego; *Bag him*! When, after ten circles or so, I realize I'm not gaining a foot on the facile upstart, I can only slink away, hoping nobody else witnessed my embarrassment and wondering where I might buy a cup of hemlock.

My own apprenticeship was much more according to form. I recall a sparkling afternoon at Chester in the spring of 1967; I had just been approved for solo in one of Bermuda High's 1-26s, and cleared to stay up as long as I wanted to. After three consecutive tows to 2000 AGL, promptly followed by ear-popping slides straight back to the airstrip, the irony of staying up "as long as I wanted to" began to reach me. Dejectedly waiting for my fourth tow, I glanced up and counted a dozen sailplanes wheeling toward the top of the sky. "Just my rotten luck," I mused, sympathizing with myself as only I can.

Like most newcomers to the sport, I was convinced it was all a game of chance, with no good cards coming my way. [Of course, there's every reason to believe I had been dragged through two or three good thermals on each tow that afternoon, but I was too dumb to know it. Further, at each release, I was probably no more than a half-mile from some other sailplane climbing briskly in solid lift—which I also ignored. I only had eyes for the pellet variometer on my own panel, the little red marker welded to the top of its tube as I carefully explored the sink between patches of green air.]

There is a tendency to dwell overmuch on luck throughout our soaring careers; it offers such an easy explanation for everything that happens to us, especially in competition. While I'd be the last to deny that luck is one of the big factors, for better or worse, in any soaring flight, I've noticed how consistently that sometimes Lady smiles on the better pilots, year after year. I've also noticed—with my cynic's eye—that bad luck seems much easier to diagnose than good luck: Losers have bad luck, winners have skill.

The luck factor in competition cannot be pinned down for analysis; it's one of those elusive, subjective forces that quite likely comes out of our own noggins rather than from some powerful eminence Up Yonder. When you wake up with a nosebleed, cut yourself shaving, have a spat with your wife, step on the cat's tail, and discover a flat tire when you start for the airport, the psychological stage is all set for a truly grisly afternoon in the air. Call it metaphysics, call it psychosomatics, or simply call it luck—but on this benighted outing, you are going to be so out of tune with the universe that dogs will howl and the sun may eclipse.

Beyond doubt, flukey weather and inept task-setting—alone, or in combination—tend to inflate the luck factor. If we are blessed with a day strong enough for a 300-kilometer speed triangle, yet the organizers call a faint-hearted 100-kilometer goal-and-return, luck is all but guaranteed to outweigh skill. Flying a short task on a strong day, a good pilot can be dumped out of contention if he reaches just one thermal a bit too early or a bit too late.

Then there's the oh-so-familiar phenomenon of over-development clamping a turnpoint minutes after the earliest starters have reached it. Such things cannot be accurately forecast, of course; they just happen. And so a lot of competent pilots find themselves milling around midway along a course leg, unable to reach the next turnpoint because of an impenetrable thunderstorm which eventually absorbs all the energy in the area and decks the lot of them.

In international competition, such days are devalued by the scorers, which seems fair enough. (And yet . . . is it possible some of those early starters moved out on the strength of a private intuition, an educated hunch? If so, then devaluation robs them of properly earned points; a ticklish decision, either way.)[1]

Whatever we choose to call it, of course there's luck in soaring. There was, for instance, the fell day at Marfa during the 1969 Nationals when eighty pilots had to negotiate the notorious sinkhole near the town of Kent. George Moffat, the day's winner, fell out of the sky like the rest of us on this miserable leg, surviving only by grace of a save at 700 AGL. Now George likes to create the impression that all his flights are totally preplanned, with every possible contingency covered in advance. But I'd bet my Social Security that until he found that thermal at 700

---

[1] In the continuing debate over how best to de-luck contests, perhaps the most promising suggestion to date is automatically to eliminate each pilot's worst daily score from the cumulative totals. The pilot whose worst daily tally is better than 900 points (out of the possible 1000) is still obviously going to be the winner. But the fellows who got trapped by a thundershower on the second leg of the third task would pick up positions on the final scoresheet that more fairly represent their flying ability than their luck. Something for the rule-makers to ponder.

feet near Kent, there was damned little icewater in his
veins. There were several of us, crossing the same area at
about the same time, who did not locate a thermal at 700
AGL or any other altitude; almost before we knew it, our
day's flying was done.

More than five years later, I'm still not certain what
factor separated the sheep from the goats that afternoon in
West Texas. Had I been the only one to blow it, I could
readily swallow inexperience, bad judgment, poor tactics or
whatever; but I had some distinguished company on the
ground with me that day. I am ready to concede that many
of the pilots who survived Kent and went on to complete
the task deserve credit for superior skill, airmanship, tactics
and other sterling qualities; obviously, they flew a hell of a
lot better than we did. But to preserve what's left of my
self respect, I must stubbornly insist that a few of them
were just plain lucky.

While only one serious mistake can ruin your chances in
modern competition, it doesn't follow that one magnificent
flight will keep you in contention. There are some famous
names who almost always win one or two daily tasks
during a Nationals, but never win a championship. When
they are good, they are unbeatable; but they don't seem to
have the concentration to fly that well all the time. With
cumulative scoring, you've got to hang in pretty close to
the top from the outset, or a thousand points on the final
task doesn't mean much.

The longer a contest, and the better it's run, the more
the luck factor tends to average out and cancel itself. When
bad weather cuts a Regional to the three-day minimum, the
lucky pilot has a good chance to beat the best one. This
can happen even at the international level, as it did in
Yugoslavia in 1972. There, the weather and the contest
organization both turned out to be dangerously sub-
standard; only the winners took the outcome very

seriously. When given any sort of fair chance, the cream usually finds its way to the top.

All well and good; but the smart pilot never underestimates the power of a gremlin; he also knocks wood, avoids cracks in the sidewalk, worries a lot on Friday the 13th, and never laughs at another's superstitions. Ben Greene once overheard me radioing to Trudy that I was on such-and-such a leg and everything was fine. After we landed, he wagged an admonishing finger under my nose: "Never say things like that! Say: 'I'm still flying, but the issue is in doubt!' " And he's so right—never ask for trouble. It's always lurking up there in the sky, eager to pounce at the first sign of complacency.

Take the one time in my lengthening quest when I thought I had a Regional championship safely in my pocket. Spring comes on slow feet to the Green Mountains of Vermont, and the last days of May in 1970 saw the birches and woodland ferns just beginning to uncurl their yellow-green foliage. For four days we had flown under claggy skies, with just enough sunlight filtering through the high cirrus to keep a contest going. Somehow I had managed to make fewer mistakes than the others, and to everyone's astonishment (mine above all), I was comfortably on top of the cumulative scores going into the final day. Whatever the task, all I needed to win was to complete the course.

Since the beginning, the Region One soaring meet has been a Jim Herman production. Jim is a great, blond bear of a man, with heart, mind, wit and soul of commensurate proportions. His contributions to the sport belong in the megaton class: he is of that vanishing species, the immensely talented pilot who is always willing to help run contests instead of always flying in them.

At Sugarbush, the briefings are staged atop the incongru-

UNSEEMLY HILARITY ON THE SUGARBUSH LAUNCH GRID

While Trudy Seibels helps stuff the author into his *Libelle*, Art Hurst's double-edged *bon voyage* provokes a guffaw. But mounted turnpoint cameras and folded sectional map (lower right) connote serious business at hand.

(Photo by Harald Krauth)

ous control tower that presides over the tiny airstrip—an open-air tradition contrived, I suspect, to cruelly discomfit any thin-blooded Rebels who stray so far north. On this, the final morning, relentless cirrus sailed high overhead in nearly solid waves; on the exposed tower roof, a persistent northerly breeze spoke bitingly of the unmelted snows of Canada, only 50 miles up the valley. I would have cheerfully settled, then and there, for calling it a contest; we could probably have reached the safety of our car before the mob caught us, and Jim could have sent me the winner's medallion by registered mail. No such luck.

Jim did call the only rational task: we would fly to the mine at Belvedere Mountain, a mere 42 miles up the valley from Sugarbush, and then fly back. *In the bag* I told my frozen self; *three thermals out, two thermals home.* And tried very hard to believe it.

About two hours later, I towed into a sky as lifeless as the catacombs. Two separate gaggles had formed over the eastern ridge, but when I found they were milling about in zero sink, I snorted off in search of a real thermal all my own. Fifteen minutes later, I was back on the airstrip, sheepishly waiting for my second tow.

This time, I inwardly snarled, *don't be so goddam choosy.* Thus, when I stumbled on a small patch of zero sink just above the ridge, I stuck with it to see what might develop. I had barely gotten my wing in it, however, when a swarm of sailplanes converged on me from all directions. Since none of us was gaining a foot, we all wound up flying at virtually the same altitude, which made for some interesting formation work. I was so busy dodging other sailplanes I scarcely noticed as one ship, then another and another quietly left the one-ring circus on the ridge, wafted low and slow across the start line, and flew off toward the north. But as the gaggle slowly diminished, I waxed impatient. By damn, I was going to find a real thermal; and by damn, I would gain some altitude; and by damn, I would make a decent start at the top of the gate, high and fast.

Well, by damn, I was back on the airport again in just ten minutes. As I rolled off the side of the runway, the mainwheel plopped into an unseen pothole; the ship stopped with awful abruptness and a fearsome sound of overstressed structure. I have mercifully forgotten my exact remarks at that trying moment; I can only recall that as Trudy arrived to help remove the canopy, Tango Tango's cockpit was turning a gaudy, Prussian blue.

I was positive I had pranged the ship right out of the contest, but a careful inspection disclosed no damage except a slightly bent axle. An old pro in the axle-bending game, I knew this could be dealt with after the contest. In the midst of a great sigh of relief, I happened to glance skyward—there wasn't a sailplane in sight! Instantly, relief gave way to a jumble of emotions, none of them pleasant: panic, outrage, frustration, self-loathing. With everyone else out on course, piling up points, here stood I, trapped at the contest site, letting victory slip away by default. Again I remembered that stupid afternoon in a 1-26 at Chester, years before; again, I simply could not stay up.

Perhaps anger made the difference. I instructed my tow-pilot to deposit me directly above the start gate. While still on tow, I radioed the gate to stand by for an immediate start. At release altitude, I simply banked to my right and was through the gate in seconds. By now, my rage had condensed into an iron resolution to fly north until I found lift or hit the ground, whichever came first.

Like a dog sniffing fenceposts, I investigated every bump I encountered, working the puniest whiffs of rising air for 50 feet, 100, or whatever I could wheedle. There was no ridge lift, with the breeze parallel to the mountains, but the high ground seemed to offer the only hope of thermals as I recalled the coffin-atmosphere over the Sugarbush valley. At wide intervals, a small rift in the cirrus would permit a few watery rays of sunlight briefly to brighten the ridge face, and after 30 miles of clawing and scratching much too close to the trees, I chanced over a small outcropping of rock that cooked up the first honest lift of the day. It was an interminable climb, never more than 100 fpm, but I was more than content to rise away from those voracious limbs and branches although drifting slowly backwards.

It was actually a miserable day for cross-country soaring. Between the pathetic thermals, there was abnormal, eerily smooth sink—some sort of wave effect, I suppose, although there certainly wasn't any compensating wave lift that I could detect. It had been an hour since I'd seen another sailplane, but as I topped one more shapeless, anemic thermal, I suddenly saw them all, circling like a swarm of albino gnats about five miles south of Belvedere Mountain. I assumed they had all made the turn and were Sugarbush-bound. Even so, they would be just one thermal ahead of me; perhaps, with luck, the laggards would conveniently spot lift for me on the ride back.

I joined the gaggle near the top, and when I couldn't squeeze another foot of lift out of the crowded thermal, I took a deep breath and broke away for the turnpoint. If the wave-sink didn't do me in, I hoped to scuttle back to the same spot after shooting my pictures. Over the turnpoint, as I dropped the left wing and tripped the shutters, I was transfixed by the spectacle of the entire gaggle, now strung out across the sky, trailing me in to Belvedere—they hadn't made the turn, after all!

That exhausted, overworked thermal south of Belvedere was still twitching when I returned, but I could feel the life draining out of it as I slowly rose once more above the forested crest. What now? Some of the pack had begun to arrive below me when I noticed a streak of sunlight gilding

a village off in the valley, a few miles to the south. The
ridges on either side were heavy with cloud shadow. With
more optimism than rationale, I headed for the village, and
this time I had no followers; the smart money was staying
on the high ground. The wave-sink intensified over the
valley, and I had a nifty little race with the altimeter,
trying to reach the warm village rooftops before I ran out
of sky. At something less than 500 feet, I passed downwind
of an ugly black factory roof and was tendered yet another
save. As thermals go, this was a plodder, but eventually it
plodded on up to 4500 AGL, a splendid altitude after
nearly two hours of hedge-hopping. But from this heady
perch, I could see most of the homeward course, due
south, and a discouraging vista it was. Overhead, the cirrus
had closed in tight; the nearest sunshine slanted 15 miles or
so to the southeast, near Montpelier. Even as I watched and
circled and pondered, a sailplane landed in a pasture close
to the ridge. I got the message, and set course for Montpelier.

On the way, I had another earnest conversation with my
Maker: "Please, Sir, I know I've been a dreadful pest today.
But if You'll let me find one more thermal, I won't bother
You any more, I promise. Amen." Because I knew that a
landing this far from the course would scuttle my distance
points—and any chance of winning.

It worked; on the outskirts of Montpelier I curled into a
gorgeous 300-fpm ride back to 4500 AGL; this, combined
with a quartering tailwind, allowed me to make a vulgar
finish, low over the tower at redline. Ever since, that final
glide has been treasured as a triumph of the utterly
unexpected over the seemingly inevitable.

Since that unique day, I hasten to add, my luck has been
averaging out nicely: good around the airport, dismal out
on course.

SERENITY AT SUGARBUSH

As the afternoon shadows lengthen over the Green Mountains, Ted Falk has just made it safely home from the task, to a warm welcome from crew and bystanders. Ridge in background is trusty site of "the house thermal."

13

A LONG DAY

Soaring and ballooning, of all aerial sports the most photogenic, have finally been discovered by Madison Avenue, and the popular press is panting close behind the ad executives. Today, the "in" way to sell cars, booze or filtertips is to pose the pretty crumpets and the product alongside a shiny sailplane, or leaning from a wicker gondola to emphasize cleavage. Newspapers and general circulation magazines, which traditionally ignore aviation except for the more spectacular accidents, have taken to running articles and features about soaring—most of them by staff writers who, alas, never before laid eyes on a sailplane.

The pictorial publicity does no harm, I suppose; after all, it's just about impossible to make a bad picture of a sailplane, even when it's sitting on the ground, cocked over on a wingtip. But the articles that accompany the pictures are often something else, usually averaging at least one howling error per sentence, all of which is duly digested and memorized by an innocent public. The most routine aspects of the sport are depicted as perilous, whereas the true risks are rarely noted; the simplest things are rendered complicated, while the difficulties are over-simplified, and the real point of the game is missed by a country mile. After constant exposure to this kind of muddled nonsense, it's little wonder that people get the notion that soaring pilots are half-heroes, half-maniacs, hazarding life and limb behind roaring towplanes for a few ecstatic moments of free flight—birdmen with birdbrains harboring a death-wish and ignoring gravity. The obligatory closing for such essays is a quasi-poetic *coda*, a sort of free-verse hymn to silent wings, the free-wheeling and untrammeled life in sunny skies, and the boundless courage of brave pilots who commit body and soul to those beautiful but fragile craft, etcetera, etcetera. Yuck!

Well, now. If some of these scriveners would only take the time to do a little homework, like having a quiet chat with a real-life soaring pilot, they might get a more accurate impression of what we do, and why we do it. An actual soaring flight from here to yonder can indeed be an enobling experience, one that nourishes the soul while caressing the aesthetic sensibilities. Maybe one out of ten, with luck.

The typical soaring flight is more likely to be just one damn thing after another. Follow me through the contest task I now recall as The Long Day at New Castle, Virginia . . .

It was late summer, with Labor Day just ahead; since the start of the contest, the weather had wobbled back and forth between marginal and dreadful. Haze and smog shrouded the peaks and valleys of the fabled Blue Ridge Mountains, murdering most of the thermals in their cradles and leaving us to grope around in borderline IFR[1] visibility. More than once, I had blundered into a thermal of sorts and made two or three circles before realizing, with a start, that I had joined a gaggle.

Ever the optimist, our Competition Director this day concocted a 192-mile speed triangle with turnpoints at Lynchburg and South Boston. The first leg would be easterly, across the Blue Ridge; the second to the south; and the third, a long, northwest diagonal back to New Castle.

[1] IFR: Instrument Flight Rules—weather that has deteriorated below the minimums for VFR, or Visual Flight Rules.

Pursuing my then-favorite notion that early starts insured early finishes, I was one of the first pilgrims through the gate. Crossing the ridges toward Fincastle Valley, I connected with a spectacular thermal which gave me an honest 500-fpm ride up to cloudbase, just under 6000 MSL. "Wow!" I said to the instrument panel; "Wowee!", and was thankful for the 150-pounds of water ballast in the wing tanks—I had very nearly dumped it on the ground before takeoff.

At 5800, I dropped the nose, cranked in negative flaps and stormed out over the valley at 90 knots. Fifteen miles ahead lay the foothills of the Blue Ridge—ten minutes' flying time. I had expected the air above the valley to be unproductive, but it was nonetheless an eerie ten minutes in that creamy soup without a single bump. Finally I could make out the first wrinkles of the Blue Ridge chain up ahead, where I felt sure the higher ground would serve me as well as the New Castle ridges.

But coming in over the hills, I could find only small patches of zero sink, separated by huge torrents of down. If anything, the visibility here was worse than at New Castle; darting from hillock to ridge in search of lift, I was soon quite thoroughly disoriented. Navigation, however, was not at the top of my worry-list just then; I faced the horrid possibility of coming unstuck at the end of my first glide.

Eventually, I found a surly patch of semi-rising air which grudgingly took me back up at 100 fpm—a far cry from the booming ride I had expected after that fine thermal near New Castle. But at least it gave me time enough to sort out my position, until at 4000 MSL the ground below began to vanish. Here, cloudbase was nearly 2000 lower than at New Castle. Oh, boy.

While climbing, I had spotted a dual line of railroad tracks—the reliable old Iron Beam—which the chart indicated led more or less directly to Lynchburg and the first turnpoint. In the pervasive murk, my best bet seemed to point toward following the tracks and hoping to bumble into lift along the way; cu's remained invisible until I was almost under them, ruling out any intelligent flight-planning. Wing and a prayer.

It was a long, tedious tiptoe, stopping to work every scrap of lift, but finally I was able to establish that the buildings and streets below were indeed Lynchburg, Virginia. Our photo target was a single paved runway on an obscure airport northeast of the city. I spent a maddening ten minutes trying to locate the damned thing in relation to the network of freeways that crisscrossed the city below. The lines on the chart and the actual freeways bore no discernible resemblance to each other—evidently, there was a terrible failure of communications between the map-makers and the highway engineers.

After much prowling about, the pictures were finally shot and I established a southerly heading toward South Boston. I was relieved to see the air ahead gradually clearing, until it was possible to identify landmarks as much as five miles away. Even the clouds began to show as separate entities, and my snail's pace quickened slightly.

About halfway to South Boston, I spotted the first sailplane I had seen since leaving New Castle: Jim Smiley's *Libelle* marking a devoutly wished-for thermal. I joined him, and together we explored what proved to be a real teaser. In spots, there was 200 fpm lift, but I could find no way to center it, so that much of each circle was wasted in down, or zero sink; we were actually gaining about 50 fpm.

All along the second leg, I had worked better lift than this, so I politely ducked out of the circle and forged ahead. In quick succession, I investigated three fat cu's that must have seen me coming; they had ceased to function. By now, I was near panic altitude—below 1000 AGL. A mile or so ahead, possible salvation appeared in the form of a tiny hamlet whose chief enterprise seemed to be an enormous junkyard covering many acres with disemboweled trucks, autos and other rusting relics, baking in a patch of bright sunshine.

I have an ironclad rule that water ballast must go below 1000 AGL; as I ran for the junkyard, I yanked the lanyard and heard the water gurgling through the dump-valve behind my head. It was still draining in a misty stream behind the ship when I sloped in over the junkyard at no more than 500 feet, and curled into a gorgeous, intoxicating thermal that took me straight to cloudbase at 400 fpm.

I was able to make fair time on into South Boston, enjoying improved visibility and reasonably good lift most of the way. Nearing the turnpoint, I noted that the cu's were becoming more scattered and flatter, without vertical development—yet it was still midafternoon in late August. "Ominous, ominous," I said to myself: "Take care, Seibels."

Banking into position for my photographs, I kept an eye on some rather decent-looking cu's just across the Dan River south of the airport; it would be worth a two-mile detour to get back to cloudbase before setting out on the final leg.

Pictures made, I turned for the line of cu's—and watched with sinking heart as they began decaying and shredding at my approach. With a sincere, "Ah, shucks!" (or something equally forceful), I swung northwest toward the center of South Boston, where a large factory was emitting a disgraceful, polluting, enticing column of smoke.

I was practically over the smokestacks before I noticed that due to some sort of local inversion, the smoke was only rising about 500 feet where it flattened into a horizontal, downwind smudge. As I crossed the factory, the air was utterly smooth. I considered returning to the airport, where I could land safely and claim two legs completed; but the lure of a few extra distance points prevailed, and spotting some open fields on the northwest outskirts of the city, I headed for them.

The nearest of the "open fields" turned out to be a golf course, with one fairway exceptionally wide and long and inviting. Gliding in above a nearby shopping center, gear down, I planned to make one low circle around the fairway to spot any golf carts (and golfers) before landing. A tiny nudge in the seat was accompanied by a weak, tentative "cheep" from the vario. Rolling into the lift, I looked down to the paved parking area that surrounded the shopping center and knew what was responsible for my last-second reprieve—if reprieve it was.

Desperately circling, shifting my centers by a few cautious feet at a time, I clung to my precarious 300 feet, neither gaining nor losing an inch. In ten minutes, I had collected a fair-sized gallery of gawkers on the ground; even some of the golfers across the road had stopped to watch— a good idea in the event I had to land after all.

As weariness and discouragement fought for control, I kept on grinding around in unproductive circles, trying to figure some feasible way to escape from this trap. High overhead, a shelf of thin stratus was filtering out most of the sun; my only hope was that a break in the cloud might drift in my direction sooner or later, letting some strong, vital sunlight through to my parking lot. So around and around we went, clutching at this broken straw.

Then, after many minutes, there *was* a patch of sunlight creeping along the ground in my direction. It was maddeningly deliberate as it slowly approached the area below, but then it flashed along my wings as the entire parking lot lit up.

I circled on for nearly five more minutes before anything happened. Then it came: for the first time in 45 minutes in that well-worn piece of sky, I got an entire circle in lift. Then another. And the lift grew slightly stronger until I was achieving a steady 100 fpm climb. At 2500 the whole thing simply died—but after spending almost an hour down on the deck, 2500 seemed like an opulent, carefree altitude. I crossed a small lake and flew in beneath some dark, shapeless clouds on the far side. After a long search that took me to the brink of despair and 1200 AGL again, I finally found the lift I was after, climbing to cloudbase at 200 fpm. The chart disclosed I was now about nine miles from the turnpoint at South Boston airport, which I had photographed exactly an hour earlier. Nine miles per hour—could I sustain this giddy pace?

But at least I was still flying, with enough altitude in hand to leave the huge sink-hole around South Boston and head for some interesting rolls of cumulus far ahead. A bit later, I could see that these clouds formed a street, and while they diverged 30-degrees to the north of my proper course, they offered a juicy opportunity to make up some lost time without too great a distance penalty. I tucked in under the edge of the cloudmass, cruising slowly at first while regaining lost altitude, then near cloudbase I set the flaps for a 90-knot run.

I had some happy minutes up there, muscles untensed and nerves calm for the first time since the flight began. As reference points showed up, my thumb slowly moved along the chart, parallel to the straight courseline; we were eating up the miles.

Inevitably, it came to a sudden end. The big bank of clouds took a sudden, right-angle turn to the north; it would be pointless to follow them farther, as I'd be getting no nearer home.

Flying due west, now, to return to courseline, I could see a flash of water—Smith Mountain Lake, about halfway between South Boston and New Castle. I began to toy with the notion I might make it all the way, especially as the last cu's in the sky were dead ahead. I was further encouraged when I found Joe Conn's big *Cirrus* circling under the nearest cloud. I joined him at the same altitude and slipped into his circle. After a turn or two, I was puzzled; neither of us was gaining a foot. His thermal had evidently lapsed into zero sink. A mile or so ahead, a sister cloud showed its dark, fat bottom provocatively. Leaving Joe in his patient circle, I scuttled away to the promised land, dropping a few hundred feet in the process. Coming in beneath the dark mass of cloud, I waited expectantly for the vario to shout the good news. Nothing. A sweeping circle around the upwind edges. Nothing. A hopeful probe to the downwind side. Violent sink. I had been had.

Somewhere on this side of the lake, there was supposed to be an airport; if I could reach it, the retrieve would be greatly simplified. If not, there were plenty of open fields a half-mile or so back from the lake's shoreline. I turned back on course, skirted a small ridge, and slowly glided along, buying a few more miles with my remaining altitude.

In a field just ahead, I saw a farmer loading haybales onto a wagon. A recently-mown field is usually a safe haven; I headed for it. Gear down once more. And once more, this time at barely 200 feet, I felt a promising little nudge along the wings. It took two or three circles at breath-holding altitude to center the thing, after a fashion, but what I had was indeed a fifth-rate thermal.

When I was satisfied I had things under control, having climbed perhaps 100 feet, I was astonished to see Uncle Joe gliding in below me. He had quietly followed me from that last, futile brush with the phony cu, and was now sharing the only lift for miles around.

Moments later, a third ship flew in from nowhere and joined up overhead: Vic Peres in his *Kestrel*. After the flight, he told me he was under 300 feet when he came in. I was below him, and Joe was below me!

With each circle, the big *Cirrus* at the bottom of the
stack would gain slightly on me; no matter how I concen-
trated and coordinated, Joe was climbing through me. Soon
he was even with my little *Libelle*, then above me . . . 100
. . . then 200. Suddenly I found I was no longer climbing
at all. Adjust each circle as I would, the thermal at my
level had simply quit. Meantime, I saw Joe and Vic slowly
dwindling into the sky above. I had been robbed in broad
daylight!

Bitterly cursing the two of them, cursing myself, cursing
the sport of soaring and everyone connected with it, I
collected my miserable 500 feet and slunk off toward
Smith Mountain Lake airport, which I could now see
through the trees ahead. On the way in, I paused to claw at
a couple of bumps—by now a reflex—but it was no use; I
had spent my day's quota of saves.

A few minutes later, I stood beside *Tango Tango* on the
airport, radioing my downfall to Joe, who kindly passed
the word along to Trudy so the retrieve could start moving.
Both the *Kestrel* and the *Cirrus* were back at good altitude,
came Joe's cheery report. I ground my teeth and declined
to acknowledge. (Peres was one of the three finishers for
the day; so was Smiley, who won the task at 40 mph.
Uncle Joe couldn't quite hurdle the last ridge going into
New Castle, landing five miles short of the finish line. I
salute them, one and all.)

I had flown 310 minutes that long afternoon; something
close to 300 of them fell considerably short of my original
conception of what soaring should be like. To be quite
honest, it had been drudgery, not fun; and when it finally
ended, I was exhausted physically, squeezed dry emotional-
ly, and to this moment I cannot think of one worthwhile
lesson I learned from the entire dismal day.

Ah, to soar like a bird, carefree and untrammeled,

dancing lightly along the sloping winds and surging currents of the heavenly oceans, silent wings buoying a joyous heart!

Any well-fed bull could do better than that—and he wouldn't need a typewriter, either.

14

SOME LIKE IT HOT...

There's something special about West Texans, there really is. Oh, sure, I've yawned at all the clichés about the tall, quiet men of infinite courage and fortitude who carved cattle and oil empires from the hard grit of the barren lands West of the Pecos. Judging by those I've met, the clichés are true. There must be some quality of that harsh, rock-hard environment that produces a uniquely level gaze, a firm grip, and a whooping, hell-for-broke approach to everything they do. Flying with them, drinking with them, just *being* with them, you get the feeling that life is somehow larger, richer and more rewarding than you thought possible.

Wally Scott fits the mold perfectly, although to the best of my knowledge he has no direct concern with either cattle or oil; in fact, he's in the movie theater business in Odessa. (It's rather surprising how little most of us in soaring actually know about each other's occupations and careers; unless the information is volunteered, one doesn't probe. The flying is all that really matters.) His courtly manner notwithstanding, he seems constructed mainly of spring steel and corundum; currently grounded after a near-fatal illness, he will no doubt soon be back in the air—and back in contention—with or without his doctor's blessing.

Wally doesn't bother himself much with the grey areas of life. If he likes you, you can feel a warm glow 2000 miles away. If he doesn't, you can detect the chill at high noon in mid-July. Along with these and all the other good West Texas traits, Wally has a magnificent talent for soaring, whether in the crowded frenzy of competition or out on lonely quests for new world's records.

Ben Greene, twice U. S. National Soaring Champion, so far, is unaccountably still a bachelor, so far. Beautiful women fight to be near him; soaring pilots on every continent take pride in his friendship; and while he stands close to the pinnacle of the sport year after year, he seems always to have time to congratulate a student on his first solo, counsel with fledgling cross-country pilots, and help solve problems that boggle non-technical minds, such as mine. He designs and builds his own sailplane trailers, which are promptly copied by manufacturers here and abroad. He is a craftsman and a perfectionist; you would know his immaculate ship on any launch grid, even if you didn't know his competition numbers. (I hate to get spotted anywhere near him, so unflattering is the contrast in housekeeping.)

Despite his addiction to ghastly puns, he's as good a companion as you could wish for, anytime, anywhere. Watching him fly a sailplane is both an aesthetic and an educational experience, the ultimate blending of art and science. He is that rarity in any sport, a man both modest in victory and graceful in defeat; a champion's champion.

Off and on for the past decade, Ben and Wally have pooled their formidable talents in repeated assaults on world soaring records in the goal and distance categories. When you aim at this sort of target, you are of course setting yourself up for some bitter disappointments. Ben and Wally have had their share, but it never occurred to either of them to quit.

Sunday, July 26, 1970, had been a routine summer day at the Columbus, Nebraska, airport—until late in the afternoon, when the unusual occurred: a visiting sailplane touched down on the runway after a 320-mile cross-

country flight from near the southern border of Kansas.
The pilot, Frank Lilly, was elated with his flight of more
than 500 kilometers, which wrapped up his Diamond
Badge. As the locals helped him walk his *Sisu* inside an
empty hangar, the first long rumbles of distant thunder
rolled in from a huge semi-circle of building storm cells
west and north of the field.

Bone-weary in their cockpits after nearly nine hours of
flying, two other sailplane pilots also heard the muttering
thunder and flinched at the evil flicker of lightning along
the northwestern horizon as they, too, approached
Columbus.

Ben and Wally, both aboard AS-W 12s, had towed out
of Ector County airport at Odessa that morning; it now lay
some 700 miles behind. Originally, they had hoped to
shatter two world records between them: free distance (647
miles, flown by Al Parker out of Odessa six years earlier)
and distance to a goal (641 miles, established in Europe
just six weeks earlier by the German veteran, Hans-Werner
Grosse.)

Under the game-plan, both pilots had declared
Thedford, Nebraska, as their goal before taking off at
Odessa. The crowline distance was some 700 miles,
comfortably beyond either of the existing records, and the
route from Odessa would keep them mostly over high
terrain, where the lift is normally strongest. Should both
make it to Thedford, the pilot with the least altitude would
land there and claim the goal record. The higher pilot
would press on as far north as possible, to claim the
free-distance record.

They had been waiting for weeks until the ideal weather
pattern began to develop. Now, in late July, an unusually
powerful cold front was sweeping eastward from the
Rockies across the plains. A trough between this front and
a warm air mass lying east should create helpful tailwinds

for a flight to the north-northeast, and the prefrontal convection ought to stir up some superb thermals along the proposed course.

Mostly, it turned out just as good as expected—except that the cold front was racing eastward far more rapidly than forecast. A radio check with the Flight Service Station at North Platte, Nebraska, confirmed in midafternoon that the front had already swept into the Thedford area, completely blocking it off with high winds, torrential rain and zero visibility. With the declared goal scrubbed, it became an all-out try for free distance.

Wally and Ben had launched within minutes of each other; they had been in almost constant radio contact; and they had been flying exactly the same course. Yet they had soared over eight hours and covered 650 miles before they made visual contact, converging on the same thermal near Hastings, Nebraska. Climbing together at last, they checked their charts and found they were just across the red-pencilled arc representing Al Parker's old distance mark. Radios tuned to the soaring frequency for hundreds of miles around would have picked up some wild whoops and chortles; a new record was now in hand.

From this point on, the flight became a two-man race with the weather ahead; they wanted to make the new record a real whopper. By now, the frontal zone to the west and north was well defined by a line of towering anvils which cast deep shadows eastward across their flight path. Where these shadows fell, convection ended, the air suddenly smooth and lifeless.

Topping out their long climb, the two ships pressed on together toward Columbus. The storm clouds to their left were rushing toward the warm air zone to their right, and they found themselves flying into a narrowing vee of clear air between the two colliding air masses. As the Columbus airport came into view, Ben and Wally debated their next move.

They were still 2000 AGL; in an ASW-12, with good tail-wind, this could produce at least 20 miles of extra distance with margin to set up a landing in an open field—if there was an open field handy. A local pilot was monitoring all this discussion on the ground; familiar with the terrain, he advised against pushing farther north; the countryside up there was rough and heavily forested. With storm cells closing in from three sides now, any further penetration would mean a dicey landing in rain and gusty winds, with damage to the ships a strong probability. And it was growing darker by the moment.

Reluctantly, they agreed to end the flight at Columbus, where the runway was smooth and long and there were hangars for shelter from the storms (their cars and trailers were hundreds of miles behind them, hopelessly out-distanced). It was the only rational decision.

To ensure that they would share equally in the new record and the attendant honors, Ben and Wally circled down in formation, separating only on the final approach to give each other landing room. As both ships flared out smoothly over the runway, Wally radioed a countdown: " . . . three . . . two . . . one . . . touchdown!" The handful of witnesses heard a single "Skreek!" as the two landing wheels made simultaneous contact. Then the wingtips scraped gently on the ramp as the great white ships came to rest.

The distance was officially measured by great circle at 716.952 statute miles—70 miles beyond Parker's previous record. This magnificent tandem flight was to stand unchallenged for nearly two years.

But when the challenge came, it came with a bang.

15

. . . SOME LIKE IT COLD

By mid-spring of 1972, no one had yet cracked Hans-Werner Grosse's 641-mile goal record, so the restless German decided to improve on it himself.

Consider the vast range of weather conditions that can produce record flights: midsummer in the southwestern United States, the baked and parched semi-desert spewing masses of hot air up to four miles into the sky—and the bitterly cold spring of 1972 in northern Europe, with snow flurries persisting into late April. This says something of the versatility of sailplanes, and the men who fly them.

Grosse, too, had been a faithful student of the weather charts; on April 25, he saw the day he had been waiting for. His flight-plan was to launch from Lübeck, a town some miles northeast of Hamburg, West Germany; thence to fly southward across all of Germany and France to the goal of Nantes, on the French Atlantic coast. The distance was 692 miles.

Hans-Werner's flight turned out to be oddly similar to the tandem epic flown by Greene and Scott two summers earlier. The German is also a powerful competitor with an international reputation in soaring circles; he, too, flew an AS-W 12; he took advantage of strong tailwinds; and like Ben and Wally, he also decided in midflight to abandon his goal in favor of sheer distance—but for quite different reasons.

The big 19-meter ship was launched at 8:20 a.m., and the incredible flight was underway. The hour is significant: rare is the day when sailplanes can even stay in the air, let alone barge off cross-country, before ten or eleven o'clock in the morning, especially in the spring. But Hans-Werner found the sky half covered with early, low cumulus at 2400 AGL; some were trailing snow showers, but others provided workable lift as the northeast wind drifted him past Hamburg and out on course.

Hans-Werner had been flying less than an hour when he picked up another German voice on the sailplane frequency. It proved to be Klaus Tesch, who had also been studying the weather charts, and had launched from another field near Hamburg. Before taking off, neither pilot knew of the other's plans. Tesch told Grosse that he, too, was on a goal flight—to Ancenis, a town near Nantes on the French coast, a pre-declared distance of 653 miles. Obviously, if both pilots should complete their flight plans, Tesch would have nothing to show for his efforts but a superb flight and membership in the exclusive 1000-kilometer club.

As Hans-Werner crossed the Rhineland, the tailwind had increased from an early ten knots to a more vigorous 15-20; cloudbase was up to 5000 MSL, making for longer, faster cruising between thermals. Over northern France, the lift continued excellent—up to 7000—and the wind was blowing from 30° at 25-35 knots.

Via radio, the two pilots kept each other posted on their progress; when Tesch reported he had his goal of Ancenis in sight, they recognized the possibility of shattering not one, but two world records on this astonishing day: Tesch to land as planned at Ancenis and claim a new goal record; Grosse to fly on south, paralleling the Atlantic Coast, in search of an absolute distance mark. Agreed.

The lift continued strong as Hans-Werner raced south. When he contacted another powerful thermal at 7:45 p.m., he realized he could easily make it to Biarritz on the Franco-Spanish border. From his supine position in the cramped cockpit, he was unable to make accurate measurements on his charts, but nonetheless he felt certain this flight would far exceed any previous distance ever flown in a sailplane.

With Biarritz under his wings, 2000 feet below, Hans-Werner—like Ben and Wally—toyed with the temptation to penetrate on into Spain for still greater distance. But the sun had already set, he had been in the air for nearly twelve hours, and the thought of shattering his beautiful sailplane while blundering into an unknown field in the gathering darkness compelled him to call it quits. He touched down at the Biarritz airport at 8:13 p.m.

From the point where he had released from his tow-plane to the point where he landed, the Great Circle distance was 907.7 statute miles.

Understandably, officials at the Biarritz airport were at first skeptical when Hans-Werner told them what he'd done; then, as they began to recognize the truth, they went wild with enthusiasm. The exhausted pilot was assigned an official interpreter, given private lodgings for the night, and subsequently made an honorary citizen of the famous old resort.

Thus Hans-Werner claimed his third world soaring record on his third attempt. Some years later, when he was visiting this country, an acquaintance asked him to explain his perfect batting average. Hans-Werner gruffed: "Ve only fly ven de vedder is gut."

To give some perspective on the quantum leap in pilot and sailplane performance in recent years, less than two decades ago, Dick Johnson of Dallas, Texas, was the only human who had soared farther than 500 miles. In less than 20 years, the ante has doubled; for now that Grosse has demonstrated that 900 miles can be soared in a single day, the race is on to be the first to break the magic 1000-mile barrier. Whether it will be done on another extraordinary spring day in Europe, or during a sizzling summer in the U. S. Southwest—or in the freezing winds that rake the Appalachians in the wake of an autumn or spring cold front—accomplishment of this ultimate soaring feat is at least in sight. Whoever does it first deserves a place alongside Lindbergh in aviation's Hall of Fame.

It will have to be a flat-out race against the clock; or, more precisely, against the sun. Assuming it's to be a thermal flight, it must be accomplished during the hours of daylight, and what a day it must be! To cover 1000 miles, the pilot will have to *average* 100 mph for ten hours; or about 83 mph if he stumbles onto a 12-hour soaring day, as did Hans-Werner. Current world speed records for sailplanes covering mere fractions of this distance, using only the peak hours of a strong day, scarcely match this sort of performance.

Ridge-thrashers in this country believe they have the inside shot at the 1000-miler, via the goal-and-return method along the Appalachians that parallel much of the Atlantic Coast. The same conditions that favor ridge-lift also frequently produce standing waves high above the mountain tops. Wave-lift is so smooth a ship could safely be flown at placard speed—say, 150 mph—with none of the punishing turbulence always associated with strong, low-level ridge-lift. However, waves are tricky to locate and even trickier to navigate, since they tend to follow the pattern of surface topography which creates them. They are also the offspring of high winds aloft, so that a sailplane using wave would be quartering into a powerful crosswind, which could drastically reduce its effective groundspeed. Let's rate this approach possible, but not probable.

On the thermal route, tailwinds will be absolutely essential for any chance of success; an average of 30 knots for a ten-hour flight is like a free gift of 300 nautical miles. Anything much better than 30 knots becomes a mixed blessing, since such winds almost invariably disrupt thermals, making them difficult to center. No one is going to fly very far or very fast in disorganized lift.

If I were a betting man, I'd lay my dollars on the ridge route. There are certain built-in problems, of course (it never fails). The optimum ridge conditions usually develop during the winter, when the days are shortest; this is when the huge cold air masses surge south from Canada with enough momentum to sweep clear down to Florida, insuring strong, reliable northwesterly winds across the entire Appalachian chain in their wake. If, by some freak of the weather, such a front should roar across the Eastern United States in early autumn, or late spring, on a day when 13 hours of sunlight are still available, I know certain pilots who will be hurtling along the ridge-tops as close to redline as they dare toward a turnpoint 500 miles from where they started.

May the Lord make His face to shine upon them.

16

NINE DAYS IN OCTOBER

You are slamming along at better than 100 mph in the violent turbulence close to the ridge, where the lift is strongest. Treetops race past your wingtip, less than a span away—three miles of them in less than two minutes.

A sudden, sharp thermal, torn loose by the wind from the sunlit rocks below, flings the sailplane a hundred feet higher with a force of five or six g's. Just as abruptly, the succeeding downdraft hits you with negative g's, pinning you against the seatbelt and shoulder straps. For an instant, your feet hover helplessly above the rudder pedals; you wince as the fiberglass spar-butts a few inches behind your head creak and groan under the punishment.

Up ahead, the ridgeline rises sharply to a crest several hundred feet above your present altitude. Grimly you bore straight ahead until your nerves protest that you're going to crash headlong into the rocks and scrub. At the last second, bare yards from the threatened point of impact, you feel the fresh surge of lift as the wind responds to the terrain, and the ship responds to the wind, magically climbing as the ridgeline climbs. You are exhilarated, like a man who has just been shot at—and missed.

For eons, the great soaring birds have known all about ridge lift—especially the birds of prey: hawks, eagles and the like, and the huge condors that inhabit mountainous terrain. Instinctively they seek out the upwind slopes, even sheer cliff faces, where they know they can lock their powerful wings in soaring position and cruise for effortless hours while scanning the valleys below for the furtive movements of fresh food. Only when the breeze dies altogether must they labor with flapping to stay aloft.

Amateur pilots began discovering how to fly with wind and ridge in the German Alps during the 1920s, back when gliders were evolving into sailplanes and the sport of soaring was almost a German monopoly. For years afterwards, all soaring flights were made in the high country; ridge lift was the only known way.

Finally, someone worked out a technique for thermal soaring (which the soaring birds had also understood for eons). The ridges were largely abandoned to wildlife as glider pilots embraced the heady freedom of soaring anywhere the sun chanced to heat the earth's surface.

In recent years, the wheel has come full circle again. A few adventurous American soaring pilots have been exploring the ridge lift along the Appalachian Mountain systems, in search of new world distance records. *Seek*, the Book says, *and ye shall find.*

Any flight in the vicinity of the Appalachians is a fair test of a pilot's pucker-power. I have flown short portions of the route on badge flights and in competition, and there's never a dull moment. For me, the dividing line between excitement and sheer fright is always blurry when I'm storming along a ridge crest with no possible escape-hatch should the breeze subside. The total dependence of soaring pilots on natural forces over which they have not the slightest control is perhaps the chief attraction of our sport; it is the common source of our moments of joy when we prevail, and our moments of terror when we don't. And in ridge-soaring, we literally cast our fate to the winds.

Karl Streidieck was the first modern U. S. pilot to mount a serious assault on the ridges. With his wife, Sue, he lives in a secluded farmhouse atop Bald Eagle Ridge, where the Allegheny portion of the Appalachian Mountain chain bisects Pennsylvania. There's a reasonably smooth meadow nearby, which they call "Eagle Field," whence he launches his sailplane for epic travels to the southwest and to which he returns after successfully completing one of his flights to a goal and return. Sue usually tows him aloft with a cable attached to the farm Jeep. As soon as he's a couple of hundred feet above the meadow, he releases the tow cable and glides over to the upwind face of the ridge. If there's enough breeze to produce soarable lift, he's off and running. If not, he sadly circles down to the valley floor and picks a fallow field for a landing strip. Then the ship is derigged, stowed in its trailer, and trundled back to Eagle Field to wait for a better day.

Karl made his first spectacular run on the ridges in March, 1968, when he somehow coaxed his slow-flying, low-performance Ka-8B to complete a 476-mile goal-and-return—a new world soaring record. Subsequently, other pilots flying far more sophisticated equipment periodically upped the distance figure, and the record shuttled between several nations. Wally Scott eventually recaptured the honors for the USA in August, 1970, with a 534-mile thermal flight in his big AS-W 12.

By this time, Karl had traded up to an AS-W 15, which he flew to a new goal-and-return record of 569 miles in November, 1971. About a year later, New Zealander Dick Georgeson, flying a 19-meter *Kestrel* mostly in wave, pushed the distance just beyond the 1,000-kilometer mark with a 623-mile flight Down Under. Inexorably the stakes were pushing higher. Karl waited impatiently for the autumn winds to begin their steady sweep across the ridges, generating the day-long lift he would need for a really long flight. He began pestering aviation forecast offices day and night.

Like most accomplishers, when Karl determines to do something, he goes after it with ferocious intensity. He was now totally committed to the ridge-soaring game. As a fighter pilot with the Air National Guard, his training missions allowed him to study all the possible ridge-routes from 30- or 40,000 feet. He also flew all the alternative courses in slow lightplanes, at low altitude, noting the exact elevation of every ridge-crest, charting every possible landing site, measuring the gaps between ridge-ends where he would need help from thermals; planning, figuring, thinking. He was learning by heart every slope, every hamlet, practically every yard of the course he planned to fly in the fall.

Always there are the trees. They have conquered the ridgelines, and they own perhaps 85 percent of the valleys below. There are 20- and 30-mile stretches in these mountains where you won't find a single acre of open, level ground. Should the wind die and the lift fail here, you are simply doomed. Even if you survive the crash-landing among the leafless, hardwood trees, your chances of reaching help are not reassuring. You think to yourself: those who shed tears over the shrinking American wilderness ought to take a gander at the Appalachians—from the air.

Striedieck was awake at 5 a.m. on October 6th, 1972. Through his livingroom window, he watched a heavy drizzle falling from the low overcast that obscured even the nearest ridges. The cold front that would bring in its wake the reliable northwest ridge wind was slower-moving than forecast; he had to wait until after 8 o'clock before the ceiling lifted enough to permit a Jeep tow from Eagle Field. Dodging in and out of the scud along the ridgetops, he headed SSW toward Altoona.

At the Altoona Gap, the clouds were again below the ridge crests; Karl sawed back and forth along the lower slopes, hanging on for an hour before he could climb high enough to jump the Gap and press on. From Altoona south to his declared turnpoint at Tazewell, Virginia, the weather slowly improved. Cloudbase rose to 6000 and there were breaks now in the overcast. At 1:30 that afternoon, he banked into a steep left turn on the far side of Tazewell, clicking his turnpoint cameras—the halfway mark.

Bitter cold, hostile terrain, painful turbulence, along with the dominant fear of damaging the beloved ship, and the subordinate fear of hurting yourself . . . scarcely ideal components for a day-long flight. Let your mind wander for a brief moment, and you can find yourself in severe trouble. Often you are flying too close to the trees and the ridge to dare glance at a map; you rely on memory and intense concentration to navigate these look-alike ridges for hundreds of miles.

Tightly strapped into the tiny cockpit of a high-performance sailplane, you can almost count the hours by the intensity of the aching, burning pressure-points on your body. A tiny lump in the parachute behind your back becomes a device of exquisite torture . . . a seat-cushion that slips a half-inch forward exposes your coccyx to direct jolts from the unyielding fiberglass seat; it will be a week before you can sit down again without wincing.

You glance at your wristwatch and realize you haven't seen an open field large enough for an emergency landing in 15 minutes. But the lift is still working, so you shrug.

A bit later, you flip your radio receiver over to the Unicom frequency just for the comfort of hearing a human voice. But after a few monotonous seconds of listening to Cessnas on downwind and Cherokees on final, you find it distracting and you return to the silence of the glider frequency.

As Karl retraced the miles on the return leg, he found the winds gradually backing around to the northwest, so that they now flowed perpendicular to the ridges: the ideal situation for maximum ridge lift. He describes the trip home as "uneventful"—which means that as he soared along at 80-100 mph, a few feet away from the highest trees, his body absorbing its accustomed savaging from the turbulence, he was no longer terribly concerned about staying up.

More than ten hours after taking off, and less than 45 minutes from sunset, Karl at last saw the familiar outline of Eagle Field framed in his canopy. Lowering his landing gear, he cracked his spoilers and flared in for a smooth landing.

He had flown a great-circle distance of 636 miles, set a new world record, and joined the exclusive 1,000-kilometer club. That, he thought, ought to hold 'em for a while.

But glory is notoriously fleeting, as Karl can eloquently confirm. For this was the start of the Nine Days in October.

Down south in Clover, Virginia, Jim Smiley had been studying "Striedieck's Ridge," too, and to him it looked like a two-way street that could be tackled from the south end as well as the north. He was also getting on a first-name basis with the weather people, and he saw his big chance two days later, on October 9th.

Just 49 hours after Striedieck's take-off from Eagle Field in Pennsylvania, Jim was on aero-tow in his H301 *Libelle*, climbing up from the airport at Bluefield, West Virginia. Releasing from the towplane, he headed for the ridge where he found a steady breeze kicking up enough lift for him to maintain altitude while cruising between 90 and 110 mph. He had also done his homework, mentally checking off the passing landmarks without unfolding a map.

Whenever he reached gaps in the ridges, strong thermals

showed up right on cue, enabling him to climb well above the ridge-lift so he could glide across to the next link in the chain. The weather was treating him kindly, it seemed. But he noticed that the wind velocity was increasing; so was the turbulence.

Jim's turnpoint was a dam near Lock Haven, Pennsylvania—325 miles from his release point at Bluefield. He reached it in five hours, averaging 65 mph on the outward leg.

Back on the ridge again, and by now it had become truly rough. The ride back to Bluefield took just four hours (better than 80 mph), but the punishment was brutal. "It was like somebody beating you with a two-by-four," Jim remembers, "for several hours."

Then, in something of an anticlimax, he had to hold on the ridge for 45 minutes while his wife rounded up some people to witness his landing. In his elation over smashing the two-day-old record with a 650-mile flight, Jim scarcely noticed the bruises and sore places; but for several days afterward, he could barely move, and it was a full week before the pain of his battering began to subside.

Those Nine Days of October reached their climax the following weekend. Karl had to spend the week flying professionally, fuming over his usurped record. He had developed a rather proprietary feeling for his ridges, and the fact of another pilot's topping his triumph (albeit a close friend) rankled. He would have another go at the first sign of decent weather. The forecast for Sunday, October 15th, was promising.

This time, Karl was joined by Bill Holbrook—veteran soaring pilot, instructor, competitor—who had never flown an official 500 kilometers to complete his Diamond Soaring Badge. Karl, of course, had his sights on bigger game: a 680-mile out-and-return, with Rosedale, Virginia, as his turnpoint.

It turned out to be a wretched day for ridge soaring. The wind was weak, variable and unreliable; thermals were few and far between, and long before reaching Rosedale, both ships were close to landing several times. Both pilots readily admit that had they been flying alone, they would have abandoned the project early in the day. But together, they radioed encouragement to each other, helped one another find lift when things got desperate, and egged each other on "a few more miles"—and finally they both had Rosedale in their camera viewfinders. Here, Holbrook could have landed honorably and claimed his Diamond Distance, but Record Fever was beginning to raise his temperature, too. Why not share this one with Karl?

The long struggle back to Pennsylvania was a mirror-image of the flight south, with the same weak spots in the ridge-lift, the same gaps that had to be hurdled with whatever thermals they could find. And now the day was fast fading, with the narrow valleys already in deep shadow.

Holbrook, unfamiliar with this terrain, prudently decided to land while he could still see well enough to pick a good field. He touched down at 6:51 p.m. after covering 657 difficult miles. (And because his barograph[1] had malfunctioned, he couldn't even claim his Diamond Distance, after flying more than twice the 312 miles required! The rules are firm.)

Karl, meanwhile, knew the ridges near his home well enough to risk an after-sunset approach to Eagle Field. He landed safely around 7 o'clock after twelve interminable hours in the cockpit and undoubtedly the toughest flight of his soaring career. And his barographs were working perfectly; he would claim the third world soaring record of that fabulous October fortnight on the Appalachians.

---

[1] Barograph: a device that measures and records altitude on a slowly revolving drum. The resultant trace is called a barogram, and must be submitted in support of claims for F.A.I. Badge or record flights, mainly to prove the flight in question was continuous. There are a few cheaters in every crowd, alas.

Through the winter of 1972-73, Bill Holbrook was host to a raging case of Record Fever. His flight with Karl had sold him on the necessity of meticulous planning and advance preparation. He spent the long winter developing a detailed flight plan designed to demolish every existing cross-country soaring record but free distance: 783.2 miles from Lock Haven, Pennsylvania, to Hansonville, Virginia, and return. (The actual distance covered along the winding ridges would be 816 miles, but point-to-point great-circle distance is what counts.)

Bill calculated he would need a 12-hour day to cover that much terrain at an average groundspeed of 70 mph. An abortive attempt was made on March 19th; and although he did cover 70 miles in the first hour, his *Libelle* took on so much ice he was forced to land at Altoona at seven in the morning. A fast trip, but a short one; valuable lessons were learned, however, and the flight plan was further refined.

Chuck Lindsay, whose help Bill had enlisted for his record attempt, phoned Bill that May 5th looked like a winner on the prog charts. Pilot and family drove to Lock Haven on the night of the 4th, while Ed Byars flew up with Bill's towplane.

At 6:02 the next morning, Bill was rolling down the runway with full ballast tanks behind the SuperCub. A few minutes later he was whistling along the crest of Bald Eagle Mountain at 100 knots, flying through snow flurries under a low ceiling. The snow soon ended and the ceiling began to rise as Bill flew southwest.

It was to be a classic day. Ten- to 15-knot winds across the ridges, handy thermals of better than 1000 fpm wherever he needed them to jump the gaps, beautiful visibility. With NASA-like precision, he reached his turn-point only four minutes behind his flight-plan schedule.

For the happy pilot, the trip "home" was equally

CHAMPION RIDGE-THRASHER

Bill Holbrook, as of this writing, has flown the longest ridge-flight of them all (783 miles), and the second-longest soaring flight in history. Next, 1000 miles?

delightful. The ridge lift was so strong he could cruise near redline several hundred feet above the crests, almost free of the punishing surface turbulence below. He enjoyed flying right through a local soaring contest at his hometown of Cumberland, Maryland, with all the pilots on the glider frequency cheering him on his way.

Near Altoona, Karl Striedieck was enjoying some local soaring (despite a rotten head cold that should have grounded him for the day); he joined up with Holbrook and gallantly flew close formation with him almost all the way into Lock Haven. When Bill obviously had it made, Karl wished him Godspeed, sneezed, and turned back toward Eagle Field, while Bill prepared for a triumphant landing.

Reaching behind his head for the knob to jettison his water ballast, Bill found it had been knocked off the valvestem by one of the bigger bumps en route. Small matter: just make a good, smooth landing so the extra weight in the wings wouldn't strain anything. (But what if he had been forced to land in some rough pea-patch?)

And so it ended—for the time being. Holbrook's was the second-longest flight ever made in a sailplane (the longest, to date: Hans-Werner Grosse's 1972 Trans-European free distance flight of more than 900 miles). He had clobbered Striedieck's latest goal-and-return record by better than 100 miles. Barographs, turnpoint cameras, documentation—all were in perfect order.

It will be a tough record to break; but the planning is already underway.

17

ALWAYS A BRIDESMAID

It was one of those rare bluebird days in the eastern United States. A bustling cold front had scrubbed the sky clean of noxious fumes and particulate matter; at 5000 you could see the humps of the Great Smokies, looming sharp and crisp a hundred miles away. The sunlight burned pure white through the crystal air, slamming into the earth below like a friendly laser beam; the soil sizzled and kicked West Texas-style thermals back into the Carolina sky. Cu's sprouted in every direction, beckoning to infinity.

Six of us were flying out of Chester that afternoon, racing from one cloudbase to the next, romping along at 85 knots in a loose, spreadout formation, burning off 2000 or 3000 feet with each run, relaxed in the knowledge that the next thermal would take us back up at 700-fpm or better. Slightly ahead of me was Ben Greene's Standard *Cirrus*. His wings flashed sunlight as he knifed through the turbulence, then went pewtercolored in the dense shadow of a cloud 2500 above us. On he raced for five, ten, fifteen seconds, the rest of us converging on his trail, then finally he arced up in a wide, climbing turn that smoothly tightened around the core; he continued upward at nearly 1000 fpm. One by one, the rest of us flared into the magnificent thermal, until all six were spiraling together toward cloudbase.

This was pure fun-flying—no scoring, no awards, no formal task to be flown. Yet for these pilots—Ben, George Squillario and the rest of us—competition and flying are as inseparable as breathing and life. Without really thinking about it, we instinctively try to outclimb and outcruise and outthink each other whenever we fly. It's a friendly war-game, tacit and informal, whereby we help ourselves keep intuitions alert and flying skills scalpel-sharp. It is enormously challenging—and so much fun that, once tasted, flying at any lesser level of effort and precision becomes boring and insipid.

I have come to believe that when you want to learn something worthwhile about a sport—when you are serious about improving your performance—you must always make a point of playing with people who are better at it than you are: a small fish in a big pond is the more attentive student. Only by soaring with the best in the game can you learn how quickly a thermal circle centered 20 feet nearer the ideal can put the ship below you on top. Of course, no one ever masters it all, and you should be prepared to spend the rest of your life studying the subtleties of efficient thermaling; no two thermals are exactly alike, and the perfect climb has not yet been recorded.

Yet thermaling is kindergarten at recess compared with the skills required for high-efficiency inter-thermal cruising. Suppose in the course of a 2000-foot climb, you wax an inept competitor by a generous ten-percent; you can storm out from cloudbase while he still has 200 more feet to climb. But then, let's suppose you storm straight into some heavy sink, which the guy with two left feet somehow contrives to avoid when *he* exits the thermal: things will be quickly equalized; or worse, he may end up with an inordinate, unearned advantage.

If I could trade off ten-percent thermaling efficiency for a guaranteed ten-percent reduction in the sink I normally trap myself in between thermals, I'd run around the hangar three times for sheer joy. Most thermals, once located, can be dealt with in a straightforward, manly fashion. You simply keep adjusting circles toward the strongest lift, and there you are. Cruising, for most of us, is more like a losing game of blind-man's-buff; since there's so rarely a reliable clue as to the best path to follow from one thermal to the next, we just bull ahead, generally, playing it by ear and the seat of the pants.

On some blue days, I have noticed that up near the top of the lift you can see hazy, almost milky protrusions poking up through the inversion layer; this phenomenon is highly visible through Polaroid sunshades, and can only be caused by thermals stronger than the average for the day. When there are a lot of them, you can porpoise along the tops for many a carefree mile while lesser mortals grind around in circles far below, hating you to the depths of their souls.

When the cu's on a given day prove to be reasonably honest, with genuine lift beneath them, they are often worth a considerable detour from the neat line on the map, if such is necessary to make the best use of them in cruising. It's much jollier, I think, to angle in to the turnpoint or goal from cloudbase, albeit eight or ten miles off course, than to know it's dead ahead if only you could see it through the trees. Newton, by extrapolation, teaches that when the lift is strong, so is the sink; but in practice this may be truer for the hardnose, straightline navigator than for the experimenter willing to prowl around a bit, seeking the lazy man's path. Altitude conserved while cruising obviously doesn't have to be regained in the next thermal; it's like having money left over on the 31st of the month. When you are good enough, or lucky enough, to make this system work for you, you can afford to be much more discriminating in the selection of the thermals you *do* work. There's nothing more maddening than having to accept a raggedy-assed 100-fpm thermal on a 500-fpm day simply because you've floundered through so much sink you no longer have any say in the matter—like having to order milktoast at a three-star restaurant. Of course, it happens to all of us.

If there's anything good to be said for joining a gaggle
elsewhere than at the top, it is the opportunity you get to
watch the higher people as they reach the summit and
storm out on course. If they seem to be running into
unusually vicious sink, you simply pin a note to your
mental bulletin board to take a somewhat different heading
when your own turn comes. A quarter-mile difference in
track can put the cagey pilot onto a street of zero sink
while others about him drop earthward like polished stones.
While cruising, we naturally watch each other like hawks to
make sure nobody gets to enjoy a good thermal all by
himself. But it can also be enlightening to compare sink-
rates as you bucket along with a clutch of adventurers.
There's no way a pilot can disguise the discovery of a street
of lift, and if you're not doing at least as well or better,
then the hell with pride and enterprise—snuggle in beside
him. There's no flattery like imitation.

"Hey, Gren, we're your friends!" complains the radio,
jolting me out of my ruminations to the realization that
I've led five other ships under three dead cu's in a row, and
we're now embarrassingly low for such a splendid day. I
spot a high wisp, and as we veer toward it, it begins to
fatten. A few moments later, I'm curling into the freshborn
thermal with the varios almost pegged, compensation and
all.

Ben, ever the first with a word of cheer, chortles: *"This
one's a Coke!"* (Chester-talk for "the real thing.") We are
climbing far beyond the Broad River, some 30 miles west
of the Chester airport. Someone suggests: "You guys want
to fly up to Gastonia and make it a triangle?" "Okay,"
"Suits me." The rest of us click mike switches in agreement.

And suddenly, it's a *bona fide* race. As the last ship
climbs to cloudbase, we spread out in another rough line

abreast that rapidly widens as each pursues his own scheme for traveling to Gastonia in a hurry. A few miles north of courseline, a likely-looking street of cu's lures me in that direction; another *Libelle* keeps me company. When I next look for the other ships, they are lost to sight.

Across a ten-mile stretch of empty, blue sky we trade altitude for distance until we reach the first cumulus, which is already decaying—no lift here. If the rest of those lined-up cu's are as sick as this one, we have a problem. Gliding down through 4000 MSL, the sink is becoming a worrisome thing: 3-400 fpm, with occasional dips to 600. Our little two-plane section is still flying line-abreast, a quarter-mile apart. We slip under the next cu at opposite ends of the cloud, then bank toward each other, exploring for lift. I'm still exploring when the other plane rolls into a climbing turn; at the half-circle, he's still going up—another Coke. Then I'm zooming into the lift until I'm just 50 feet below him, with both varios in the high country as the audio signal keens away. We're back in business.

Gastonia, spread just east of Kings Mountain, now stands out clearly on the horizon as we circle upward. Dark splotches of cloud shadow mottle the earth ahead like a natural dotted line that leads almost straight to the Gastonia airport, our turnpoint. Perhaps a fellow could afford to abandon the climb before reaching cloudbase and scuttle straight in to Gastonia, porpoising along beneath that string of cu's without running around in circles.

The other *Libelle* is still circling slightly above and just ahead of me; apparently, he doesn't notice when I ease out of the thermal and start running northeast—or is it simply that he is smart and I am not? It's a gamble, of course; if I'm wrong, I could end up sitting on the ground while he soared smugly overhead. But if I've guessed right, I may be on my way back to Chester while he's still approaching Gastonia.

In the sink between the clouds, I have to press hard: 90 knots, not the *Libelle's* most profitable airspeed. Drag and sinking air, between them, are costing me 700 fpm; but when I reach the next cloud in the chain, I rejoice in the discovery that I can zoom up into the lift, slow-fly for a few moments, and regain most of my altitude before nosing over for the next run. After four or five of these cycles, I am crossing the Gastonia airport only 500 feet lower than when I broke off the conventional climb. And here, through the good offices of some undeserved miracle, I blunder into a clear-sky thermal so powerful the ship goes momentarily out of control, my knees slamming against the instrument panel and my head banging against the canopy as we pass through the monstrous lift into the sink beyond. Wheeling around, I tackle it with relish: this should be the go-home thermal that ties a blue ribbon around the whole flight.

Slam-bang! Here it is again; full aileron can't force the wing down into that boisterous swoosh of sunpower invisibly boiling skyward; yet even skittering about the edges of this monster, I am climbing at more than 800-fpm. After some earnest Indian-wrestling with stick and rudder, I finally establish a reasonably stable circle at about 50° of bank; the varios are now pegged again, and even my ears tell me we are achieving better than 1000-fpm. High overhead, I can see the first flecks of cloud boiling around on the tip of this geyser; by the time I get there, a minute or so later, the sky is blotted out by the vast, black cumulus bottom, steeply domed at its center. Riding up inside this dome for another full circle, I am 500 feet above the scud streaming down from the edges of the cloud.

This is 7500 MSL—high enough to lay the tail over the dashboard and cut for home. I'm beginning to sniff a wee triumph—beating the lot of them, not by a paltry few seconds, but by long, insulting minutes.

Then the radio, silent for the past 20 minutes, brings me George's familiar voice: "Ben, did you leave Gastonia when I did?" Ben: "You bet, partner."

Leave Gastonia? How could they have gotten there, and left, before I did? Driving home at 85 knots, the flags are suddenly limp, the bubble burst, the crest fallen. I had been so *sure* I was 'way out front!

Partway along the final leg, I spotted a sailplane far below me, moving very slowly toward Chester. Then another, and a third; I was quickly overtaking them. Finally I spotted a fourth ship, separate from the others, also headed home. With my huge altitude advantage, I would surely get back before any of them, but at best I figured the winning margin would be a couple of minutes.

They didn't see me as I flew overhead and left them behind. A few minutes later I was flying at redline, a thousand feet above the fields and trees, the big triangle of Chester airport some three miles ahead. Gritting my teeth against the turbulence, I whistled across the airfield boundary, crossed the finish line at ten feet, and burned off the airspeed climbing back up to pattern altitude. My finger touched the mike switch to announce "Tango Tango finished," when I heard the best news of the afternoon on my speaker.

"You got anything there?" asked one of the competitors still out on course. "Not much, but it's better than landing," came the reply. So they were stopping to thermal! Reinflate the bubble! Unfurl the flags! Raise that crest! When I overtook them, they were even lower than I thought!

I keyed the mike, with a mighty effort to sound nonchalant: "Tango Tango finished about 30 seconds ago."

There was quite a pause while I threaded my way around two trainers in the pattern and lined up on the grass between the paved strips, easing the bird down with a touch of spoiler.

Then, "Any witnesses?" from one of the circling gaggle
behind me.

"Everybody here at Bermuda High," I chirped as the
wheel met the grass.

I was well into the tall, cold beer Trudy had brought me
when the others came hissing across the field in a tight
pack. My erstwhile companion of the second leg didn't
show up for almost an hour, after a long scrape near
Gastonia. The whopping thermal that wrote my ticket
home must have pooped out by the time he got there—
fortunes of soaring! Whether by good management or good
luck, there's really nothing like being in the right place at
the right time.

In practice, I am one hell of a flyer. Always a bridesmaid
. . .

18

MR. SMITH

I had just released from the towplane and was groping my way through the eastern Ohio smog when from behind a huge, white shape hurtled past my wingtip, then zoomed up over me in a graceful wingover. It was an AS-W 12 with a tall, skinny "2" painted on the tail—A. J. Smith. At the apex of his wingover, he flipped a sardonic little salute down toward my cockpit, and was lost behind me. A. J. was stating, in his own fashion, that he could fly rings around me.

Conceivably the world's worst team flyer, this extraordinary man epitomizes the soaring pilot as a loner. On the ground as in the air, he guards his privacy with fanatic zeal; solo is his creed and his style. At international contests, he flies to beat his own teammates along with the rest of the field, a trait that has scarcely endeared him to colleagues on U. S. soaring teams. But if he's aware of the hostility, he gives no sign that it fazes him. He is the most completely competitive person I have ever known, in or out of soaring. The intensity of his determination to win is awesome to behold.

Since greatness is relative, comparisons are in order. The only pilot in modern competition with a track record better than A. J.'s is George Moffat. Superficially, the two might appear to have much in common: superb intellects, personalities both complex and enigmatic; they thrive on competition and they fly solely to win. But if we focus beyond these facile generalities, we find they share little beyond American citizenship and an uncanny talent for victory.

George's approach to flying is dispassionate and cerebral; for him, it's mostly a game of the mind played in physical space, like three-dimensional chess. Willpower, psychology and naked intelligence are his preferred tools; he uses them to calculate and analyze and compute with a ferocious concentration that demoralizes, and eventually devastates about 95-percent of the competition. The rest he simply outflies.

A. J. also brings to competition an intellect of enormous force; in top form, he deduces ways to hurry across the sky at speeds which leave the rest of us gasping in disbelief. There are times when he seems to organize the atmosphere to his own purposes, intuiting invisible streets of lift in which he cruises great distances at high velocity while his inferiors toil in gaggles far behind.

But coupled with the keen brain is a potent emotional mechanism. Prior to his best flights, A. J. psychs himself into a towering, Old Testament wrath that can immolate his entire crew along with careless bystanders. In this volcanic state, as he once put it, he's ready to take off and "go like stink." When he manages to get all these volatile factors in just the right balance, the man is unbeatable.

Clearly, this is no league for the casual competitor; he will find himself far beyond his depth. There are probably no more than a dozen pilots throughout the world capable of sustaining performance at this level, and they are the ones who make life interesting for the Smiths and Moffats. All the rest would gladly settle beforehand for a spot in the top ten, or even the top twenty, thereby removing themselves psychologically from serious contention.

Championship flying demands a total commitment to winning; nothing less will do. It requires a willingness to accept any sort of personal sacrifice while competing— Moffat has won two World Championships while gravely ill; A. J. underwent exquisitely painful surgery on the eve of the Internationals in Yugoslavia.

THE SWEET SMILE OF VICTORY

A. J. Smith has just earned another 1000 points and now
addresses himself to charming a radio interviewer. Comes tomorrow,
and all will be business again. One of soaring's most intriguing
personalities, and a tiger's tiger in competition.

Of course there is no single key to the mystery of winning, but certainly attitude is a vital factor. The pilot who thinks, "It would be nice to win," has no chance at all against the pilot who believes, "I'm going to win." A. J. categorizes the former group as "flower-watchers;" Phillip Wills calls them "romantics," and defiantly counts himself among them. Unhappily for them, and perhaps for the whole sport, they are anachronisms; modern competition has passed them by. They persist in flying for the fun of it, for love of the game; they compete under a gentleman's code which forbids any word or deed that might possibly discomfit a fellow pilot. They are truly ornaments to the sport; but of course, they never win any more.

A fascinated A. J.-watcher, I have concluded that he is something of an anachronism, himself: the complete Renaissance man four centuries out of context. He burns with that hard, gemlike flame to excel in everything. An architect, he has earned a national name and sufficient fortune to semi-retire at an age when most professionals are just hitting their stride. I have seen him doodle design ideas with a da Vinci hand, casually tossing off pencilled gems that a machinist could use for shop drawings. Unlike many soaring pilots, his broad flying skills qualify him to solo anything with wings. (He was among the first invited to fly the prototype of Jim Bede's BD-5J, a squirrely little jet designed for homebuilders of unlimited wealth and courage.) When he's away from the psyched-up tension of contests, birds are reputed to flutter down from their trees to bask in his charm. It was largely thanks to his powers of persuasion that NASA began to apply its vast technical resources to some of the classic riddles of sailplane design and soaring flight. To describe him is like counting the facets on the Kohinoor diamond.

When talking with A. J., I often sense that he is merely skimming the surface of his mind out loud, while underneath a lot of sophisticated machinery is going "Clicket-y-clickety-hum," independent and oblivious to immediate surroundings and other ephemera. At first acquaintance, I gathered he knew more about me in ten minutes than I would know about him in ten years; an impression that persists.

Even in the best of health, he contrives to project the hypochondriac's aura of fragility—calculated, no doubt, to mislead the naive and lull them into foolish overconfidence. Totally counterfeit, of course. Perhaps he fattens up between contests; I don't know. When a championship is at stake, he pares down to minimal bone, muscle and nerve. There is an ascetic glint in his eye, which flares to a wicked glitter as the daily battle approaches. Finally tucked into his cockpit, a faint smile may briefly quirk the corner of his mouth (if his crew have done their work well); and until his flying's done, that will be the day's quota of mirth and jollity.

The compulsive competitor tends to develop a callous immunity to all but his monomania, and woe to anyone or anything that threatens distraction. By withdrawing to his quarters, pulling up the drawbridge and slamming down the portcullis, A. J. neatly escapes the social entanglements of contest nights. But there is no escaping involvement with the ground crew, and except when they are unusually ept, A. J.'s crews are likely to become grist to A. J.'s mill.

This abrasiveness with his people sometimes exceeds any accepted bounds of propriety; his tongue can cut like an acetylene torch. Many of his colleagues find this sort of behavior unforgivable; and by any normal standards, of course it is. Yet, when one is reaching for the summit, can normal standards still apply? Few have tried it; few are qualified to judge.

To those who habitually quit climbing before reaching the top, who have no heart for the passionate gamble that goes with winning, who have never blazed up in the furnace of competition, who are satisfied to settle for genteel mediocrity ... A. J.'s rage to win is alien and disturbing and almost beyond comprehension.

Absolute purity of purpose can be a devastating quality. We rarely see it, and when we do, we are not quite sure how to react. Which may explain why the world has felt compelled to slay most of its saints. (I do *not* suggest that A. J. is a saint, nor that the world is likely to destroy him. I do think he may have a similar problem in communications.)

Ever the loner, A. J. rarely appears on the launch grid until a few minutes before his takeoff time. The rest of us may be desperately trying to soothe our jitters with limp jokes and trivial chit-chat. A. J. doesn't *want* to relax; he flies best when he's uptight. God alone knows what this does to his stomach and his nervous system throughout a long, major contest. But it's his personal price for a chance to win, and he pays it without murmur.

In the air, he seems fitted with a vision denied lesser mortals, discerning in clear, blue skies waves of up and down; he makes his own clairvoyant decisions, flies his own inspired patterns, and produces flights that are a scathing indictment of the rank and file. He may flatter you by checking your thermal for a turn or two, but unless it's the genuine article, he will shimmer and disappear over the horizon while you are still congratulating yourself on showing A. J. the way. Ha.

As long as he chooses to fly, he will be a supremely dangerous adversary. If you think otherwise, fly with him sometime—and learn the full meaning of humility.

19

THE BEAUTIFUL PEOPLE

JOE'S DIAMOND

Joe Giltner has paid his dues to soaring—many times over—with untold hours of instructing and check-rides at Bermuda High Soaring School. Were all his former students to stage a reunion, they'd have to rent out Texas to handle the crowd. He was also the key in establishing Chester, South Carolina, as one of the prime competition sites in America, setting a standard for ground and launch operations that has become the perpetual envy of other contest managers.

Joe might have continued along these lines until he became the world's hoariest instructor, but for two events: one summer, on an impulse, he trundled one of Bermuda High's 1-34s to a regional contest at Cordele, Georgia, and there discovered how exciting life can be beyond the confines of the traffic pattern; and soon after, he acquired a half-interest in Morris Kline's H301 *Libelle* (officially, 5-Uniform; colloquially, 5-Ugh); one of the best ever built.

Most of us have no real defense against the charms of our first high-performance sailplane; nor did Joe. That fall, he hung up his instructor's cap, retired from Bermuda High, bought out Morris's remaining interest in the ship, and set forth to have some fun with soaring while he was still sound of wind and limb.

Soon his face became familiar on the competition circuit, both Regional and National. After all those boring hours orbiting the airport in the rear seat of a 2-22, he had much to learn, and much to unlearn; but there's fighter-pilot blood in his veins, pumped by a naturally competitive heart. He was a quick student.

Between contests, Joe's dream was to complete his Diamond Soaring Badge. One spring day he caught the elusive wave over Mount Mitchell, North Carolina, and came down with a Diamond altitude gain on his barograph. Next, he laid out a 300-kilometer Diamond Goal triangle from Chester and went charging forth whenever the weather showed the slightest promise. There were some discouraging failures, followed by some heart-breaking near misses; and then, at last, he made it all the way—only to discover an intermittent barograph trace. No trace, no Diamond.

Subsequently, Joe made several more circuits around his familiar Diamond course, but regardless of what barograph he used—old or new, borrowed or blue—there would be a foul-up. Joe had a serious discussion with a minister friend about exorcising 5-Ugh.

Then, during one of the springtime Region 5 contests at Chester—Joe's first as a competitor—he saw an opportunity and pounced on it. A speed triangle was posted that was almost identical with his own Diamond Goal milkrun; only the first turnpoint was a few miles short of the landmark Joe customarily used to make a full 300-kilometers. With the contest nearly over, and Joe no longer in contention for a top spot in the scores, he sweet-talked the Competition Director into permitting him a slight deviation from the official course, so he could first photograph the assigned turnpoint, and then fly on a bit to shoot his own, private turnpoint for badge purposes. The forecast indicated a fairly strong day.

Yet what a difference a few minutes can make! While Joe detoured to his extra badge turnpoint, the gaggle he had been flying with was moving smartly down course toward the second official turnpoint, working wispy cu's that decayed almost as soon as they formed. By the time Joe had returned to the official task course, up ahead there were neither cu's nor sailplanes to be seen. The few thermals he encountered were progressively weaker; the day was ending much sooner than forecast.

But Joe struggled on, eventually made the second turn, and began clawing his way back to Chester. If things didn't improve, he knew of a private airstrip about halfway home . . . On the contest frequency, he could hear his buddies of an hour ago calling the finish line from one mile out.

When he reached the private airstrip on the third leg, he was very low. Circling the field, he stumbled into a weak but workable thermal floating up; tucking in, Joe began to climb, slowly regaining altitude and hope. One more thermal en route would get him home. But after a long, slow, flat glide through dead air, he was doubtful about getting across the tree-lined Catawba River to the open fields on the far side. So he backtracked to the airstrip, squeaking in with just enough altitude to check on the little thermal he'd worked earlier. It was still there—still weak, but there. Patiently, Joe began climbing again. For well over an hour, Joe cycled doggedly between his airstrip thermal and the Catawba River, but never hit a bump en route.

By now, all the other contestants were either safely back at Chester, or trailering thither from the boondocks; Joe's was the only sailplane still flying. The word had spread about his badge attempt; we all crowded around our radios to see what would happen. Joe's running account of his ups and downs began to dwindle, and then there was a long period of radio silence. Since there hadn't been a wisp of convection around Chester for a good two hours, we reluctantly began to conclude that Joe had probably landed. But as people began leaving the field, Joe's voice was heard again:

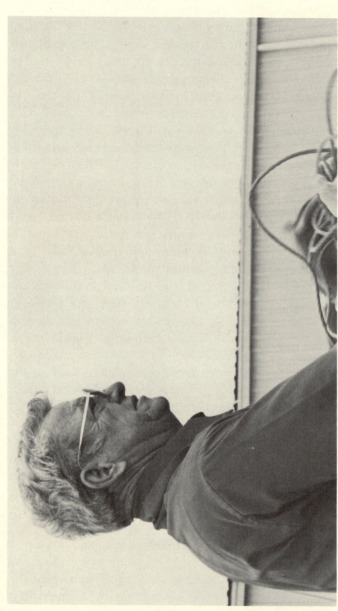

END OF A JINX

Undone by a succession of barograph failures, Joe Giltner finally won his Diamond Goal during a Region Five contest at Chester, S.C. During 1975, he flew creditably in both Standard and Open Nationals. Giltner soloed the author in sailplanes in 1967 after a scant 25 minutes of dual time; Standard Operating

"Five-Ugh's at 5000 . . . I think I can make it!"

Whoops and cheers echoed across the airport; and a short while later, Joe's *Libelle* was red-lining past the finish stripe, then landing and rolling to a stop amidst a throng of applauding friends. It may not have been Lindbergh arriving at Le Bourget, but the spirit was the same.

This time, Joe's barograph actually worked.

ICE

His was the kindest face I have ever known. When I think of him, I have this tendency to smile; he was always smiling, and I guess it's still contagious. Too, he was the best listener in the world. No matter how tedious your anecdote, he would hang on every word, nodding complete agreement and approval, never interrupting.

He was so goddamned nice I used to kid him about it. "In real life," I told him, "you probably boss all the rackets in Pennsylvania—dope, gambling, prostitution, extortion. You save up all this nice-guy stuff for soaring contests!"

Frankly, when I first flew with him, he was a pretty dreadful soaring pilot. He and his family turned up at Chester for one of our first Region Five contests, innocent and friendly as a basket of puppies. He could just barely thermal in those days, so he spent a good deal of his time scratching around at unwholesome altitudes; and when he *did* get up, he was incessantly on the radio with some weird code that told his crew his position, altitude, and for all I know, the state of his nerves. But behind all the mistakes you sensed an iron determination to learn and improve.

Learn he did, and improve he did—so successfully that after a couple of seasons it was hard to remember that he was the same guy who used to fall out of thermals and get lost ten miles from the airport. Suddenly his name began

appearing up amongst the top-level scorers in every contest
he entered—and he entered everything in sight.

There was nothing secret about his love of soaring,
either. Back in the easy-going days before the rules required
that you turn in your landing card immediately after
finishing a task, he used to burn across the finish line after
a four- or five-hour mission, catch a thermal in the pull-up,
and enjoy another hour or so of local soaring before calling
it a day.

When you beat him on a task, he would praise your skill
until you squirmed with embarrassment; if he beat you, he
would almost blush, and actually apologize for his dumb
luck. We flew in a lot of contests together, and as time
went on, his "dumb luck" was outflying my "skill" with
increasing regularity. While I can't pretend I have ever enjoyed losing, there was no way you could resent his winning.

I couldn't count the times I've recognized his voice on
the radio, reminding a competitor to retract his landing
gear. Of course there's a firm rule against this sort of
sporting gesture, but no contest official ever persuaded him
to observe it.

Instead of the killer-instinct which some consider the hall-
mark of winners, he stoked himself with pure enthusiasm.
I believe the realization that in competition, *everyone* can't
be a winner caused him genuine pain.

I can hear him now, describing one of his superb flights
at the next pilots' meeting: "I was about halfway along the
first leg, and I really needed a thermal; I happened to
glance up, and there was old Gren *zooming* into the sky—
just what I was looking for! Then, right after the turn,
good old Ben got me out of trouble again—gee, but he can
find good lift! Then I wasted an awful lot of time at the
second turn—thought I'd blown the whole thing; I wasn't
getting anywhere—when a couple of *Cirruses* came along
and led me to a real boomer, and it was an easy final glide

home from there. If all you experts hadn't been out on course yesterday, I'd never have made it back!"

So said the winner who waxed every man-Jack of us.

I can also hear that booming greeting he gave any competitor who wandered into the coffee shop for breakfast during a contest: "GOOD MORNING, EAGLE! Boy, what a MARVELOUS flight you had yesterday! Come have breakfast with us and tell us how you did it!"

Once, a sleepy-grouchy waitress whispered to Trudy, "Is that guy always this happy in the morning?" "Always," Trudy confirmed.

After every off-field landing, he insisted on locating the property-owner and pressing a lot of dollars into his hand; goodwill for the soaring movement, he explained. A friend once said, "Geez, can you imagine the reception you'd get, landing in a field he's used?"

He was still in his young fifties when he sold out his electronics industry and retired, planning to devote the next few years almost exclusively to competition soaring. By now, he was a solid Category One pilot on the national seeding lists. In that first spring of his new freedom he raced from contest to contest, flying with great dedication and skill and joy. It was a schedule that would have daunted a man half his age, but he seemed tireless.

Then it was the eve of the National Championships at Liberal, Kansas. Under a blistering midsummer sun, he (typically) was helping erect the big tent that would serve as contest headquarters, driving stakes with a sledgehammer, when his heart stopped beating.

Quentin "Ice" Berg—gone, and our world is diminished. We all miss you, Eagle.

THE VERY OLD HAT TRICK

Big John Brittingham is a Colorado cattleman, operating

a sizeable spread outside of Denver. During the off-soaring season, he claims he reflects mainly on beef and the multiple aggravations of that volatile business. But when the weather becomes civilized, Big John addresses himself at every opportunity to soaring contests, beer and liars dice—with no special order of priority.

Somehow I had managed to fly with this delightful sportsman at a couple of U. S. Nationals without getting to know him beyond a nodding acquaintance. But when he came to Chester for one of the wettest major contests in U. S. soaring history (the 4th Standard Class Nationals of 1973), we had enough time on our hands to settle down and sort each other out, a bit.

It is Big John's personal trademark and triumph to possess the absolutely nastiest flying hat I have ever encountered, or ever want to. There is a tradition that this nauseating remnant began its career, God knows when, as a respectable stetson—the fawn-colored type favored by the good guys in Western movies. Judging by its fetid appearance today, that must have been long before the era of the Sundance Kid; it may have ridden with Cole Younger. The years since have been less than kind to it; it has obviously never known shelter from rain, snow, sleet or hailstorm. But the grisly evidence, internal and external, clearly demonstrates that this relic of a headpiece saw most of its duty during hot—*extremely* hot—weather. The festering area around the headband is blotched and stained a permanent brownish-black, as if it had been carelessly dropped into a spitoon. If that dreadful hat were tossed into a 50-gallon cauldron of pure, boiling water, it would produce a ghastly soup brinier than the Dead Sea, and more opaque than the wine-dark Aegean. (The very suggestion would fetch from Big John a mighty roar of outrage.)

On one of the rainier days at Chester that June, Big John was presiding over the Permanent Liars Dice game

that he had established in the Bermuda High hangar—
thoughtfully located within arm's reach of the beer
concession. As the game proceeded through a typical
arpeggio of unlucky rolls and outrageous lies about what
lay beneath the dice cup, with Big John alternately brow-
beating and cajoling the opposition with the forensic skill
of a slightly crooked Clarence Darrow, I became fascinated
with a huge swarm of flies which had taken refuge from
the flood outdoors, and instinctively formed a buzzing
gaggle above Big John's reeking lid. After a while, a few of
the flies—perhaps fatigued, but more likely overcome by
the fumes—began to wobble a bit, and threatened to fall
into someone's beer. Politely but firmly, I suggested that
the offensive bait be removed from John's head (sacrilege
in itself) and deposited elsewhere in the hangar, preferably
the farthest corner.

Surprisingly, John bared his head without a murmur.
Handing the hat to a young crewman who was kibitzing, he
directed him to place it gently on the wing of a nearby
Bermuda High trainer. This the volunteer did, but he
happened to set it down on the gnarled, limp shards of the
brim. Big John erupted:

"*Never* put a good hat down on its brim," he roared at
the hapless crewman, "it ruins the shape!"

Lanier Frantz shares my queasy regard for that hat. He
recalls a visit to Denver years ago, during which he received
an invitation to an extremely starchy banquet at the area's
poshest private club. Big John, his host, gave him directions
and promised to meet him there. As Lanier and his date
entered the formal lobby of the establishment and were
checking their coats, he glanced around the semicircle of
niches containing marble busts of locally famous figures.
Perched on the stone pate of one of these worthies, Lanier
noted, was that unique, unmistakable object: Big John's
incredible Nasty Hat.

"We've come to the right place," he whispered to his companion.

Big John flies with a deceptively casual, nonchalant expertise that confounds his many inferiors in soaring and baffles his few peers. Most pilots approach competition with a grim, give-it-everything attitude. John enters contests because it's the only style of soaring he truly enjoys. He's rarely in his sailplane between meets; without competition, he tends to get bored. This alone helps explain his proficiency; he never dulls the keen, competitive edge, as most of us do, by waffling around the local gliderport while our reflexes rust.

What's more, Big John refuses to take competition seriously except when he's actually flying. After completing a task, as he generally does, he thrives on massive infusions of beer; after nightfall, he will share harder waters if that is the will of the group. He considers the evening wasted unless a half-dozen companions gather for conviviality while lesser men force themselves to an early bed, there to toss and agonize over the known mistakes of the day and the unknown mistakes of the morrow. While others grapple with sweaty nightmares, Big John and his coterie laugh and carouse and discover one another's good points. It's really not a bad way to get through a contest.

He is a prudent, brainy, superbly coordinated, highly aware flier. Sailplane performance means little to him: he has as much fun winning the 1-26 Nationals as he does placing regularly in the top ten at the big Open or Standard contests. He entertains no compulsion to win, only to fly reasonably well (which, in his case, is a good deal better than most)—and above all, to enjoy the whole thing to the utmost.

If Big John ever gets as serious about winning a soaring contest as he is about dominating a liars-dice table, he just might topple some of the most famous crowns in the sport, both here and abroad. But no, his idea is simply to do something enjoyable with enjoyable people.

When a man genuinely holds the act of soaring itself more important than winning or losing, yet consistently frazzles the front-runners, I think it says something hopeful about the future of the sport.

Pity there aren't more like him.

THE SUN NEVER SETS

John Hearn, the Baltimore radiologist, is a transplanted Briton who retains every nuance of that lovely, precise British manner of pronouncing our Mother Tongue. I doubt that any active conspiracy exists between John and his fellow soaring émigrés—Graham and Helen Thomson, Erica Scurr and the rest—to recolonize the States, or even to reform the inhabitants, but within their spheres of influence they do exert a most civilizing effect on our speech. To hear any of them converse is literally music to my ears.

Like most of us, John tends toward slightly cockeyed adventures in his sailplane. One sample:

"Around most of the triangle, I'd flown extraordinarily well, until this blasted patch of cirrus invited itself into the sky. You know, there's really nothing good to be said for cirrus. Of course, at this juncture, everything came unglued. I got down well below a thousand feet and had quite made up my mind to land, when I found a lovely bit of lift and began working it for dear life. I was just beginning to climb nicely with every circle when along comes this helicopter chap to see what I'm up to. Next thing I knew, the silly bastard was hovering right overhead—and he SQUASHED my THERMAL! Quicker than Bob's-your-uncle, I was on the ground!"

John flies mostly out of Frederick, Maryland, where

hangar space for sailplanes seems to be at a premium. He told me of the sad occasion when he was driving the shards of his broken *Phoebus* back to Frederick after a vigorous off-field landing on the final task of a Regional at New Castle, Virginia. Switching on his ground station, he listened in on the airborne chatter of some of the Frederick locals until he recognized the voice of a close friend. John called him on the radio and as he motored along, told him the grisly details of the accident.

When John finished his tale of anguish, the friend's response was:

"What a pity . . . Er, John, you won't be upset if I apply for your hangar space, will you?"

SHORT HOPS

Ben Greene tells a story from the Age of Wooden Sailplanes:

A hapless pilot had committed some grievous error of judgment and slammed his brand-new *Austria* into a Vermont hillside, reducing it to an expensive stack of kindling, but without serious injury to himself. The remains were tenderly stowed inside the gleaming trailer which was then parked outside the inn where the soaring gentry had gathered for the weekend. For the bereft pilot, Saturday evening was a long, lugubrious affair. After a quantity of Scotch-on-the-rocks, he felt the urge to step outside and commune silently with what was left of his gorgeous ship.

As he approached the parked trailer, from inside he detected strange yet somehow familiar sounds; the sounds, in fact, of enthusiastic lovemaking. Wrenching open the trailer doors, he glared down on the couple, stark naked amidst the wreckage, and roared:

"My God, have you no respect for the dead?"

Ben also told me of the venerable competition veteran of the early postwar era who decided a few years ago to come out of retirement, briefly, for one more fling in a National Championships. With 60-plus sailplanes cluttering the contest skies, and pilot-crew messages flying like shrapnel on the contest frequency, the old-timer's voice suddenly dominated the airwaves with this bulletin:

"My dear, do you remember where you bought the banana you packed in my lunch? It's really not quite as good as the one you bought yesterday.

"Do you think you could find a better one tomorrow? This one's a little past its prime; there are brown spots in some places . . . . " and so on and on.

After "my dear" had duly acknowledged this critique and promised to do better on the morrow, the airwaves were eerily silent for long moments. Nobody could think of a damned thing to say.

Not all the fun and games occur in the sky. Our old soaring chum, Morris Kline, happened to be First Man Up one Sunday morning when a group of us were weekending at the Chester Motor Lodge. There ensued a lot of enthusiastic pounding on doors, as Morris made certain all his friends would join him for breakfast. George Squillario had overslept, so Morris offered to place his breakfast order for him in the dining room. George ordered a routine breakfast, but without juice.

"No juice?" asked Morris, in a pained voice.

"No juice, thanks," responded George, firmly.

"Aw, come on, George," pleaded Morris. "Juice is some of your best friends."

Of all the soaring anecdotes, I suppose my favorite remains the dilemma of a pilot, flying in one of the Elmira Nationals, who realized he was utterly, hopelessly lost above the unfamiliar ridges in the summer haze. He was also familiar with the inflexible rule that prohibits pilots from seeking any sort of help while flying a task; but when he spotted his car and trailer parked on a knoll directly below him, he had a crafty inspiration. Calling his ground station, he ordered his crew to "Say your position."

Back came his wife's cheerful voice: "We have you in sight, dear; we're right below you!"

Trudy still chuckles wickedly over a radio transmission of mine during a recent Region Fiver at Chester.

Our errand took us to the eastern sector of the task area, where we found a high overcast drifting relentlessly across the courseline. Flying through mile after mile of dead air, with no visible source of lift ahead, it occurred to me that I might just possibly be confronted with my first off-field adventure in two years of conservative tactics. As often happens, I had taken off without a nickel in my jeans, much less my wallet full of credit cards. I tried hard to remember our current telephone credit code suffix, but my mind was too busy with other matters, such as survival. Now it's bad enough to squash a portion of a farmer's spring crop; I could never muster the gall to place a long distance call at his expense, to boot.

"Hello, Squaredance."

"Squaredance," replied my ever-attentive crew chief.

"Honey, what's the final letter on our telephone credit card?"

"E, as in Echo," she responded, between spasms of irrepressible mirth.

Much later, when a few of us had contrived to make it home, Ben Greene and several others who had monitored the conversation stopped by our tiedown spot as we were derigging and rolled about the tarmac, laughing hysterically; heartlessly, Trudy joined them.

Me, I didn't think it was so damn funny, then or now.

20

UP, UP AND AWAY

They hung almost motionless in the evening sky, like enormous Christmas tree ornaments in their gaudy color patterns. Of the dozen hot air balloons we had watched ascend an hour earlier, eight had floated together across a few miles of pine forest and now were slowly, slowly drifting toward open fields, the intermittent bursts of flame from the propane burners like the breathing of sleepy dragons. We three soaring pilots and our wives watched, entranced, as they bobbed gently up and down, two of the huge globes almost dragging their gondolas in the treetops, the others a few hundred feet higher. (The remaining four must have ridden different air currents aloft, and landed God knows where.)

On our way to western North Carolina for a weekend of mountain soaring, we had pounced on the chance to drop in on a balloon rally near Statesville. It was mid-afternoon when we reached the launch site, where we found a scene not very different from a gliderport early in the day, before the lift begins. Equipment was casually scattered all over the grass while pilots and crew members wandered aimlessly about, tinkering with this or that, pausing politely to answer our outsiders' questions. The little meadow, almost surrounded by tall pines, looked impossibly small to our conventional pilots' eyes; we were unaccustomed to thinking in terms of vertical takeoffs.

Then, by some secret signal, there began a bustle of organized activity, focussed first on one balloon, then another. Countless yards of synthetic fabric were being tussled and manhandled into a semblance of smoothness. At the gondola end of the bag (envelope, in aeronaut lingo), helpers held the open skirt erect so that powerful, portable fans could force thousands of cubic feet of air inside. Gradually the top of the envelope swelled and inflated, until the balloon lay bulging on its side like a beached whale. Then the pilot would light his burners and carefully squirt a few blasts of roaring flame through the skirt into the balloon's internal economy. Sheer decibels almost lifted onlookers off the ground as the BTUs began building inside: WHOOOOSH! . . . pause to note the effect . . . WHOOOOOSH! . . . and the whale began turning into a globe . . .WHOOOOSH! . . . and the globe ponderously lifted itself from the ground and rose into the air above its gondola, gently swinging like an inverted pendulum, seven stories high and 55 feet wide at the equator. The transformation took something less than five minutes.

Aeronauts, as balloonists style themselves, can create almost any color scheme they wish for their craft, and they don't seem to be terribly inhibited about bold colors. One sported a crazy-quilt pattern of at least ten contrasting hues; another came in basic patriotic red, white and blue. Some favored herringbone designs, others solid-color panels from top to bottom; there wasn't a mousy-looking one in the lot. By the time a half-dozen had been inflated and were readying for liftoff, that little grass meadow was the most colorful spot in the southeast.

Costumes for ballooning are as uninhibited as the craft themselves. A visiting Frenchman sported a furry brown beret and a sheepskin jacket lined with scarlet fleece (although the surface temperature was at least 80°). Another chap wouldn't dream of an ascension without his stovepipe hat.

Close up, the periodic blasting of the burners is truly deafening—a pity, for this may be the only serious flaw in what is otherwise the most serene way of looking down on the countryside yet devised. Since it takes several seconds for the blasts of heat to reach the top of the envelope and exert any effect on the balloon's buoyancy, a nice sense of anticipation is required at the "throttle."

Balloon instrumentation would charm any member of the "keep-it-simple" school—most settle for an altimeter and a vane variometer, usually mounted in a separate case and strapped on the gondola just before flight, to avoid damage during inflation and ground transit. Balloons are now being equipped with temperature gauges whose remote sensors, located in the top of the envelope, restrain heavy-handed aeronauts from overheating the fabric, which weakens it. Who wants to go up and hang at several thousand feet under a bag of weak fabric?

Presently most of the balloons were airborne, drifting sedately away from the field in the near-calm of late afternoon. Following in our cars, we found a road that skirted the forest and brought us to an area of open fields a few miles downwind from the departure point. The air by now was almost dead calm as we watched the eight craft probing for useful currents at varying altitudes. The thought occurred: what do they do when they're stuck over forest, there's no wind, and it's growing darker and darker? Pray earnestly, I suppose.

An aeronaut in the nearest balloon hailed us from several hundred yards away—"How about a little help?" He was slowly settling into a clearing near the banks of a stream. He then shouted directions to help us find an all-but-invisible dirt track that led to the border of the clearing where he would land. We got there just as he touched down, a hundred yards from us. Instead of deflating the envelope, as we approached he tossed us a towline and asked us to haul the balloon and gondola closer to the edge of the road, where his retrieve crew was just arriving.

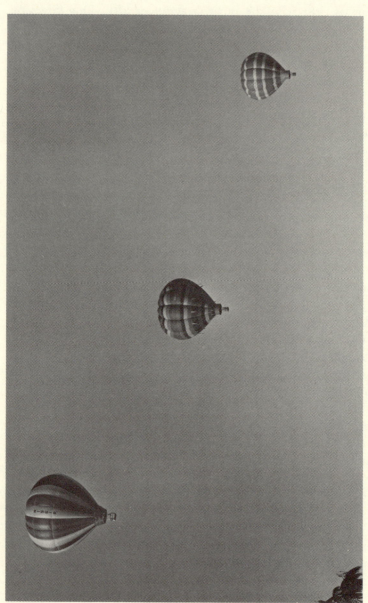

THEY HUNG ALMOST MOTIONLESS IN THE EVENING SKY . . .

Hot air balloons in a placid, downwind drift near Statesville, North Carolina. Aeronauts are as colorful as their gaudy equipment, and must brave even more off-field landings than soaring pilots.

Standing inside the gondola, using short bursts of noisy flame he kept the rig gently bobbing a few feet off the ground as we hauled him along. When we reached the designated spot, he pulled the rip panel and the great bag sighed and slithered to the ground.

The soaring group exchanged glances—each of us remembering the times when we had been forced to haul sailplanes out of isolated boondocks, component by component, with vast expenditure of sweat and energy. Maybe these people had something, at that.

At dinner that night, we were all sky-high on enthusiasm. We had found the ideal complement to soaring. Since balloons become unmanageable in thermals, operations are generally restricted to the early morning and late afternoon hours. The ideal day, we concluded, would begin at dawn with a balloon ascension, a bracing cross-country drift, and a pleasant retrieve home for a light brunch. The next four or five hours would be spent in sailplanes, flying a brisk speed triangle or two. Then, as the thermals waned, the sailplanes would land while the balloons were rigged and inflated once more for a twilight drift and a sunset touch-down—celebrated, of course, with the traditional champagne toasts. Ah, Magnolia, honey, do peel me another one of them delicious grapes, child.

I haven't made any overt moves yet, but my soul delights in the comforting knowledge that when the right moment comes along, yet another attractive (and totally useless) way of exploring the sky is ready and waiting for us.

 the Navy book), I finally began to believe the gauges instead of my panicky semicircular canals. So eventually the Navy taught me blind flying; but they never taught me to like it. Even night-flying was something of an ordeal, and still is.

And yet—have you ever seen a great city at night from the air? Years ago, I was among a group of journalists being flown to Europe by the Air Force for a tour of NATO air operations. Our lumbering C-124 had bucked headwinds all the way east from the Azores, and it was long past midnight when we made our landfall, crossing France on our way to Frankfurt. As a youngster I had visited Paris in the mid-1930s; now, 30 years and a war later, I saw that most graceful of cities again, from an altitude of I don't know how many thousands of feet. With dawn approaching, bright necklaces of light still jewelled the blackness below from horizon to horizon; the old Eiffel Tower's Victorian lines were tactfully clothed in darkness, but its lights probed the sky like a permanent Christmas tree; the Île de la Cité stood bright and aloof, moated by the inky Seine.

Although I was groggy from 18 hours inside the racketing cavern of the C-124, I stayed glued to a cold window, deep in sentiment and lost in beauty, until Paris had dwindled to a soft glow far behind.

The Navy called it flat-hatting: ripping along at full throttle down as close to the terrain as you dared. Highly dangerous and totally illegal, then as now—except that it was often called for under combat conditions; so we cadets rationalized that a bit of clandestine practice was always in order when no instructors were lurking about to put us on report. You see, flat-hatting was not only risky and illicit— it was also enormously good sport. At proper altitudes, there are rarely any reference points to give a sense of speed; at 5000 feet and 200 mph, the distant ground seems to crawl very slowly past the wings. At six feet and 200 mph, flight becomes pure speed, enhanced by the ability to zoom over any obstacle with a tiny back pressure on the stick.

Surely the Navy will forgive me, after all these years, when I admit that I have seen much of the fabled King Ranch, south of Corpus Christi, from mesquite level, flying as part of a two- or three-plane section of SNJs in tight formation. So accustomed were the Santa Gertrudis cattle to these noisy incursions they rarely bothered to glance up at us as we screamed past with props in low pitch and manifold pressures quivering on the redline. Inside our cockpits we would all be laughing with demented delight; forbidden fruit is ever the sweetest.

These exciting sins were usually climaxed by a fine, arcing climb back into the sky, 1500 feet or so nearly straight up, then leveling off and closing in tight for the trip home to Kingsville Naval Air Station, trying our damnedest not to smile like cats in a creamery—the Navy was deeply suspicious of happy-looking cadets.

Flat-hatting is highly impractical in sailplanes, of course, but we do get an occasional—and legitimate—taste of it during soaring contests, on the final glide at the end of a speed run. If we find a good, strong thermal 15 or 20 miles out from the finish line, we calculate just how much altitude must be gained to make it home at good speed— say, 90 knots. I usually take a few hundred feet extra as insurance, which must then be burned off at redline airspeed during the final two or three miles, bringing the ship down to treetop level at the airfield boundary and then on down to a yard or less above the runways until the finish line is crossed. The surface turbulence can be vigorous indeed; the price of a good finish is a lot of banging around inside the cockpit while the airframe pings and grunts and squeaks in protest. But ah, how the ground rushes past as we hurtle across the finish line! Then we pull up, converting speed back into altitude so we can land where we choose. It is a very pretty thing to watch—but that is absolutely nothing compared to the fun of doing it.

Low-altitude fun and games aside, I think the best part of flying is also the most obvious: being able to look down on the world. There may be some kinky symbolism involved here, but I'm much too busy looking at the sights to worry about it. Both with and without a throttle, I have been privileged to explore and poke and prowl over some of the most beautiful land and water in America. I have feasted my eyes on virgin forests so remote they have never heard the whine of a chainsaw; flown amongst the cruel, tortured, magnificent stone architecture of the High Sierras; studied the hot pastels of Mount Livermore, towering above the parched desert plateau of West Texas; I have seen the evil glitter of black swamp water through moss-hung cypress (and shuddered at the thought of a forced landing in such a place); and I have dipped a wingtip into powder-puff cumulus—all grey, swirling vapors at close range; and

I HAVE DIPPED A WINGTIP INTO POWDERPUFF CUMULUS . . .

The author's 1931 Great Lakes biplane skirts a classic cu. Converted to a 165-hp Warner Superscarab radial, the little white plane with blue trim has won many trophies at Antique Aircraft fly-ins, but its true *forte* is aerobatics.

have ridden thermals into the murky depths of building
cloud-castles, using needle, ball and airspeed to hold the
sailplane in a shallow climbing turn while the altimeter
leaped upward at a crazy rate—eventually escaping from
the clammy gloom into a high sky of incredibly deep
blue—and danced my way back down through dazzling
cloud canyons to the unwitting world below, performing
slow, silent wingovers and lazy-eights and rushing loops,
with the demented laughing delight of those long-ago cadet
days.

Landing, finally, a friend helps detach the canopy and
asks, "How'd it go?" Offhandedly: "Pretty good." But my
friend is a flyer and a sensitive one; he knows from the
irrepressible smile that I am just returned from secret
pleasure domes; some of that crystalline air still sweetens
my lungs; and my soul is somewhere back up there at
14,000 feet.

The Federal Aviation Administration tries to ignore us;
newspaper editors fulminate against us; most professional
career pilots consider us a damned nuisance; and the
general public misunderstands, and hence distrusts us. All
because we regard aviation as a sport instead of a business;
because we don't fly for a living, we fly for fun.

I suppose there are only two basic ways to look at
airplanes. Sensible people regard them as efficient transportation—the best means yet devised for traveling from here
to there in a hurry. Whereas romantics like me find them
fascinating in their own right, worthy of study, respect and
affection. To the practical-minded, aviation is only a means
to an end; to us romantics, it's an end in itself.

It is understandable, if regrettable, that professional
pilots tend to drift into Category One—gruff-and-grim souls
for whom flying has become all business and no art, each
flight a series of tedious checklists and humdrum proce-

dures, with only a rare surprise to ruffle the monotony. No more challenge, no more adventure, no more magic; I do not envy them.

I have lost track of the number of takeoffs I have made since the first one (good Lord, was it actually 35 years ago?); even so, as the wings shoulder the last few ounces of weight and I sense the wheels rising from the ground, I still marvel—every time. And I realize, after all the long millenia when men stood on the ground and stared longingly at the wheeling birds, dumbly wondering what it was like to be up there, how lucky I am to have been born into the first century of human flight.

Like millions of American boys growing up in the 1930s, I had squadrons of model airplanes in my bedroom, and huge stacks of magazines that dealt solely with aviation. By the time I wangled my first actual flight, I was like someone who has memorized a symphony from recordings before attending his first live performance; I was more than ready.

Then, as now, I had my share of relatives and friends who nurtured no love of flying and were baffled by anyone who did. It is a difficult thing to communicate; as sports writers all learn, there is a vast abyss separating spectator from participant, and words make but a fragile bridge. You can watch a pilot going through an aerobatic routine, trying to imagine his sensations and thoughts; but unless you have tried at least some of those maneuvers yourself in a similar plane, you'll probably miss much of it and be wrong about the rest. (Unless the aerobatics are going extremely well, most of the pilot's thoughts would be unprintable even in this permissive age; and he is far too busy concentrating on line and symmetry to notice the g-forces at work.)

Quite properly, authorities have managed to erase nearly every trace of fun from business, commercial and military aviation. Properly, because it's no time for high-spirited,

boyish pranks when you're shooting a carrier landing in
several tons of jet fighter on a rough sea; likewise when
you're driving a 747 down the glide-slope in heavy soup,
with three or four hundred sets of white knuckles trying to
trust you.

As planes gain in speed and size and utility, they inevitably become more complex. Seat-of-the-pants, wind-on-the-
cheek flying was what they mainly taught student pilots in
the 1930s; but it was a nearly-forgotten art ten years later,
so rapidly did the war catalyze the advance of aviation.
Piston engines peaked out with triple-row radials that could
deliver more than 3000 brute horsepower to the propeller.
(To take off, you locked the tailwheel so it couldn't caster,
cranked in full right-rudder trim, and as you roared down
the runway you stood on the right rudder pedal and prayed
nothing would happen to start a swerve to the left, or you
would surely buy the farm; such was the torque.) At speed,
fighters and bombers alike were chiefly flown with trim
tabs—the direct control forces being considerably more than
the average man could handle.

Today, serious (read "commercial") flying must be done
strictly by the book—although it's more like a five-foot
shelf, what with chunky operating manuals, briefcases
bulging with charts and approach plates and enough
miscellaneous reading matter to make the modern cockpit
resemble a technical library. It takes a college-level course
in communications to master current radio procedures, even
though electronic wizardry has finally cleared the guesswork
from aerial navigation—as long as the radio gear is functioning. Further, panels now swarm with new instruments,
many so sophisticated that only top-shelf professionals
really know how to use them effectively. All of this is
dedicated, of course, to greater reliability and safety, and a
very serious business it is, indeed.

But it is light-years removed from the kind of flying that

is done for the sheer fun of it, mostly in little aircraft with rudimentary instrumentation—a few simple gauges to measure such basics as airspeed and altitude and rpm's. Here, our hands and feet are directly, intimately linked to the control surfaces through taut cables and pushrods (not an unfeeling complexity of remote relays and solenoids and servos), so there's always a lively if wordless dialogue back and forth between pilot and aileron, or pilot and elevator. Such little craft tend to bob and bounce in turbulence like a cork riding rapids, making for queasiness in the passenger seat; but dear hearts, they are such sweet fun to fly!

This delightful rapport between man and machine unfortunately seems to get lost as the equipment grows larger, heavier and more powerful. Even in unpowered sailplanes, size apparently destroys feel; friends who fly the big Open Class ships, with wingspans of 66 feet and up, tell me they handle like scows. My first sailplane was a Schleicher Ka-6, a lovely 15-meter creation of thin German plywood and shiny white fabric; ready for flight, it weighed not more than 400 pounds. Although my tall frame was miserably cramped in its fiendishly small cockpit, once airborne I rarely noticed the discomfort; I was too happy enjoying a sense of oneness with the tapering 50-foot wings that seemed to sprout from my shoulders. The ship was so responsive I usually flew it with one fingertip resting lightly on top of the stick. In two seasons, I put 400 hours on this beloved bird, with a serene sense of being at home every minute we flew together.

Not since 1940, when I began flying in earnest, have I been so bright-eyed and excited at the prospect of every flight. I used the Ka-6 in furious pursuit of FAI soaring badges, barging off cross-country at the slightest hint of thermal activity, usually landing miles short of my goal— and the nearest telephone. During those sweaty, exhilarating hours, I was learning basic lessons: where to look for the best lift under a cumulus, never to venture on the lee side of a ridge, always to trust a circling hawk (and usually a circling buzzard)—they only circle in lift; and other arcane lore of interest to soaring pilots, hawks, and buzzards.

There was a mild winter day—1941 I think it was—in Eastern Tennessee where I had persuaded the university officials at Sewanee to institute a Civilian Pilot Training Program; this day I was the first student scheduled for a solo practice hop. Shortly after sunrise, we propped the J-3 Cub to a trembling semblance of life (the engine was a Franklin of ancient vintage and 40 dubious horsepower); then I was bumping down the sod runway and off into the creamy-smoothest air I had ever encountered.

There was no breeze yet; pockets of ground fog hugged the shallow swales and lowlands of the Tennessee plains. The rising sun bounced rainbows of blinding mother-of-pearl irridescence from the motionless vapors as the little yellow plane sturdily chugged upward. What little flying I had previously done had occurred during the turbulent midday hours; now I was enchanted by the Cub's surprising stability in the motionless dawn air. For the first time I found I could complete 720° steep turns without gaining or losing altitude; airspeed control, my most persistent nemesis, magically ceased to be a problem. I had the vertiginous sensation that the plane itself was stationary; the world below and the sky above went through stately pirouettes in response to my touch on stick and rudder. I have logged some hours since that flight, but never a more delightful one.

For most people, earth-life is essentially two-dimensional: east-west, north-south. Mountain climbers and skin divers enjoy a degree of vertical mobility, but the pace is slow and the effort exhausting. (Sky-divers make pretty fair speed, but it's always in the same direction.) True, near-effortless, three-dimensional freedom is the sole prerogative of pilots, and this freedom I believe is at the heart of all sport aviation. Only the astronauts have escaped earth's gravity; but the rest of us who fly in atmosphere have at least partially solved the implacable downward pull and thereby gained a measure of freedom to explore our skies. In conventional, powered aircraft we like to give each other as wide a berth as possible; but when thermals are scarce, soaring pilots gladly share a small parcel of airspace with one another as they climb in unison aboard a rising column of warm air. In contests, when pilots do everything but sleep on a competitive basis, archrivals often meet in the same thermal and exchange a smile or a wave as they spiral upward in a helical pattern. If a pilot is known to me and I trust his skill, I am quite content to circle with only a few feet of shared air between our ships.

Most of the pilots I know are insatiable seekers after perfection. Let's face it: 90-percent of flying is no more demanding or difficult than driving an automobile on an interstate highway. Mastery of that final ten-percent is what distinguishes the superb pilot from the merely adequate. For this is the largely undefined area in which experience, technique, judgment and a true "feel" for flying combine with other intangibles in a rather sophisticated formula; when all the right ingredients are there in the right amounts, then you have one of those rarities, a pilot's pilot.

In the passenger cockpit of our Great Lakes, an antique biplane, there are no instruments of any kind. I know it's unfair, but I like to see what various pilot-friends can do with the ship when I give them the controls. I have learned that most soaring pilots have perfect coordination, even in a strange aircraft; most conventional pilots do not. When a real pilot takes over, his touch is sure, positive and smooth; his timing is such that there's no wasted effort, no lost energy, no double corrections. Lovingly handled, the aircraft does precisely what the pilot asks of it; rapport between man and machine is instant and total.

A good pilot is a happy pilot. It's easy to spot a good (happy) pilot: just observe how he handles his plane, his attitude toward it. The exceptional Navy instructor who coaxed me through primary aerobatics could con our Stearman into a sequence of half-snaps, split-S's, Immelmanns, slow rolls and the like—and when we were again straight-and-level, the recording g-meter would show scarcely three positive g's and perhaps two negative. His touch and timing were those of a piano virtuoso. It was not until many years later, when I commenced re-teaching myself some of the simpler aerobatics in the Great Lakes, that I came fully to appreciate the man's artistry. The Lakes is 'way yonder more tractable and maneuverable than any Stearman, yet even so I sometimes pull four g's while practicing.

Hemingway wisely observed that the best things in life could be spoiled by too much talking about them. But even though they keep it to themselves, I believe most good (happy) pilots share the familiar yet ever-fresh wonder of wheels breaking from the ground as we commit ourselves to wings; buildings and trees and farmland rushing beneath us and then diminishing as we climb beyond the eye's capacity to resolve detail. Once again we behold the world below: an ordered entity, a Jacob's coat of greens and fawns and shimmering blue waters stitched together by thread-like roads. We might even share an unvoiced pity for all the people down there, scuttling like crustaceans about the floor of our vast ocean of air; how can they know what they're missing?

THE TRAILING EDGE

They say some of us never really grow up; our toys just get more expensive. Could be.

When I was still very young and very small, I used to wonder: "How smart am I?" or "How brave am I?" or "How good am I (at doing things)?" Now, a half-century later, these questions still ricochet out of my head at odd times . . . like a suddenly wide-awake 4:30 in the morning, Mr. Eliot's hoo-ha time.

You can drop by the town library and find out almost anything you need to know. Anything at all, except about yourself.

Look, Trudy and I are as close as any two people on Earth; the life we share is too good to be true. We hold no conscious secrets, one from the other, for when love is true and total there is really nothing to hide. Yet there are moments of silence and preoccupation when I sense that we are now and forever two remote mysteries pulsing through our days and nights, mysterious not only to one another but to our very own selves.

To the aware mind, mysteries are fascinating, but some I think are best left unsolved—undisturbed, private and inviolate. I feel no compulsion to dissect an orchid flower, submit wine to chemical analysis, or force a rationale for every domestic mood. She loves me, I love her; what need to explain a sweet day?

Yet many of us nourish this insatiable curiosity about ourselves. I often wonder why genuine happiness, for me, flows only when I am trying to do something I don't really believe I can do. Challenge, the root of all joy? Sounds like a Nazi slogan.

Ernie Gann knowingly distinguishes between pilots and airmen. For him, pilots are those whose flying falls somewhere between mediocre and barely adequate; people with little or no feeling for the sky, and hence, little or no understanding of it.

An *airman*, on the other hand, endures his earthbound hours as a sort of penance he owes the gods in return for the privilege of exploring the sky. Such a person is apt to shun cocktail parties and similar rites of boredom, preferring the good company of fellow fliers who share his rapt preoccupation with altitude and airspeed. Only with a stick in his hands and rudder pedals at his feet does he come wholly alive; his addiction to the three-dimensional skies is deep and irreversible, with the key difference that his highs are genuine, without deadly side effects. Even on solo flights, far beyond the knowing eyes of his peers, his coordination is habitually impeccable, his altitudes accurate to the foot, and his mind ranges far ahead of his craft, as it should. He is absolutely incapable of an unintentional stall; there is more sound knowledge of flight in the seat of his pants than in all the stall-warning devices ever patented.

It has been my lucky lot to fly with such men. I now believe that in such flying, and most particularly in soaring, I may have come close to answering those little-boy questions that some of us never outgrow.

How smart am I? Well, smart enough to know that I'm just beginning to learn some of the important stuff. Not yet smart enough to make efficient use of the myriad secrets generously shared with me by master airmen . . . Greene, Smith, Moffat and all the rest. Smart enough, too, to know that life is much too short.

How brave am I? Each time, before actually flying, I rediscover the same coward that once lived in a little boy

just before an unavoidable fist-fight, or upon the accept-
ance of some foolish dare. Once airborne, I suppose I do
well enough; worry, not fear, is my typical burden. It's that
fiendish hour on the launch grid, before flying, that makes
my heart pump coward's blood and my mind fall prey to
coward's thoughts. (George Squillario endures this season of
despair by apparently taking a nap curled up under his
wing, his head pillowed on the parachute—but I've never
been able to decide whether he's really asleep. For me, this
would be tantamount to nodding off while having a tooth
mended.) Waiting to start a fearsome task is infinitely
worse than doing it.

Yet I have been known to charge into bad skies where
angels would fear to tread, let alone fly; and have paid for
my foolishness with shattered fiberglass, bone and ego.
Stupidity lurks at the far end of the bravery spectrum, and
the line is mortally thin. Now, I think I've got it pretty
well staked out; for Trudy's sake, if nothing else, I intend
never again to trespass in idiotland. Stupidity never wins
anything at all.

So, Lord knows, I'm aware of the risks. When I forego
cross-country soaring for more than a month or so, it takes
a violent act of willpower to push me back out over the
boonies again. Yet by the end of a contest, it seems as
natural and effortless as driving a car. Few of us have the
heart or the energy to fly as much cross-country as we
really should between contests. When we do sally forth, it
is generally on a very low-risk kind of day, which makes
for practice that is make-believe at best. Most contests are
flown (and won) in vile weather. Hence, the screaming
molly-grobbles out there on the launch grid before the first
task begins.

How good am I? The scoresheet ruthlessly rates me as
so-so, as if to say: "We'll let you into the top third in some
contests, the top ten in a few. If you're hoping to do any

better than that, you'll have to get yourself organized." But as losers are wont to remark, scores aren't everything. Just being *in* a soaring contest is something special; there are probably fewer than 400 qualified pilots in the whole country.

These little insights are significant to no one but me, of course. If there's anything intrinsically useful in all this, it would be that I've found nothing like flying (and especially, soaring) for opening the windows of the soul and letting you take a close-up look at what's inside. I don't like everything I've seen, by a damn sight, but I rejoice that I have had the opportunity to look.

And as long as I fly, I hope always to be probing the outer limits of my own particular set of skills, while trying to reduce the endless list of ineptitudes. The challenge is infinite: there will always be ample room for improvement. And if it comes to the point where I'm not getting any better, and I'm smart enough to notice, then I'll quit.

One doesn't talk about such things in routine hangar-flying, but I suspect most pilots who share this love of flying feel pretty much the same way. Respect is an important element of love, and we do mortally respect the sky. It, too, is a continuing mystery and thus a continuing fascination, and they won't finish dissecting it in my time.

In my time? Well, you may tell me it can't go on forever, and logic forces me to agree that you're right; but 'way deep down, I don't have to believe it.

At least, not right now.

THE END

ACKNOWLEDGEMENT

Portions of this book were adapted from articles of mine originally published in *Soaring*, the journal of The Soaring Society of America, and *National Aeronautics*, a publication of the National Aeronautic Association. To both the SSA and NAA, I am indebted for their kind permission to republish this material in the present form.

Writers moan a lot about the loneliness of their vocation; and in truth, it *is* a rather isolated experience. Yet during all these hours of solitary confinement with typewriter and copy paper, I have never felt myself without the presence—in spirit, at least—of my faithful band of encouragers: Doug Lamont, inspired and devoted editor of *Soaring*; Bill Winter, Doug's counterpart at *National Aeronautics*, who taught me so much, so patiently; Ed Byars and Bill Holbrook of *Soaring Symposia*, who stopped kidding long enough to rescue this book from mothballs; and all the loyal friends and sainted strangers who have written or voiced to me their interest. Bless them all.

Trudy contributed so much more than maps and artwork and layout. She, too, endured all the bad pages from which the few good ones finally emerged; and being the world's gentlest editor, helped me see the difference objectively, through a mysterious process of wifely osmosis of which, at the time, I was scarcely aware. Bless you, my dear.

G.S.